More than just
Coincidence

JULIE WASSMER

More than just Coincidence

The remarkable story of how a mother and
daughter were reunited in one astonishing
twist of fate

harper
true

HarperTrue
HarperCollins *Publishers*
77–85 Fulham Palace Road,
Hammersmith, London W6 8JB

www.harpercollins.co.uk

First published by HarperTrue 2010

2

© Julie Wassmer 2010

Julie Wassmer asserts the moral right to
be identified as the author of this work

A catalogue record of this book is
available from the British Library

ISBN 978-0-00-735431-3

'It's Your Thing', words and music by O'Kelly Isley, Ronald Isley and
Rudolph Isley © 1969, reproduced by permission of EMI Blackwood/
EMI Music Publishing Ltd, London W8 5SW

'Days', words and music by Ray Davis © 1968 DAVRAY MUSIC LTD
& CARLIN MUSIC CORP, London NW1 8BD
– all rights reserved – used by permission

Printed and bound in Great Britain by
Clays Ltd, St Ives plc

Mixed Sources
Product group from well-managed
forests and other controlled sources
www.fsc.org Cert no. SW-COC-001806
© 1996 Forest Stewardship Council

FSC is a non-profit international organisation established to promote the
responsible management of the world's forests. Products carrying the FSC
label are independently certified to assure consumers that they come
from forests that are managed to meet the social, economic and
ecological needs of present and future generations.

Find out more about HarperCollins and the environment at
www.harpercollins.co.uk/green

For my family

Margie and Bill
Sara
Caden and Tallulah

Two roads diverged in a wood, and I –
I took the one less traveled by,
And that has made all the difference.

'The Road Not Taken'
Robert Frost

Contents

Prologue

Close to the sea, near my home, I have a small
wooden beach hut, where I spend long summer
days with my husband, daughter and grandchildren. It
is also the place where I write. Sometimes there is little
more to distract me than the cry of seagulls and the
turning of the tide. Sitting on the verandah, looking
out at the horizon, I have a sense of completeness and
calm, of everything being just as it should be. It is a
feeling that eluded me for so long. Wherever I went,
and however happy I was, I knew that within me there
was an empty space. I was sure that one day the missing piece would be restored, but until then my heart
would never be quite whole.

As a television scriptwriter I have countless plotlines to my credit but still none so extraordinary as
the drama I experienced in my own life almost twenty
years ago: an apparent coincidence so remarkable that

many people have been compelled to search for more complex explanations as to how it could have happened.

Certainly it is hard to believe that mere coincidence could have brought together the disparate strands of my life in such an astonishing way, or provided me with the signposts that led me, at a precise time, on a precise day – 5 November 1990 – to a door on a busy street near London's Piccadilly. Even then I could so easily have turned away. But I didn't. And by crossing its threshold I came face to face with my long-lost daughter – without either of us knowing who the other was.

Two decades have now passed since that meeting. The fireworks that followed when the truth was revealed are long over but the emotions that over- whelmed me then are still just as poignant as they continue to reverberate through my life. How can I possibly describe what it feels like to abandon a child to strangers in a blind leap of faith, believing that they would be better parents than I could ever be? How can I explain the profound sense of loss; the absence so great that it becomes a haunting presence? How can I define the lasting joy brought by a reunion that seemed so random and yet so well timed?

Some have attributed this event to synchronicity, some to serendipity; others have seen it as fate. On a hot summer's day in 2010, as I gaze out from the veran- dah of my beach hut at my daughter, playing with her own two children at the water's edge, I know, as sure as my beating heart, that what drew me to her that day was more than just coincidence.

It is time to share my story.

Chapter One

Black Plimsolls Tied With Ribbon

I was an only child and likely to stay that way. My mother often remarked that, while she loved me dearly, she would have been just as happy with a litter of puppies. It was a sentiment that shocked friends and neighbours but I understood it completely: there were animal people and there were children people. My mother belonged in the first camp. For that matter, so did I.

At four years old I mothered my own 'family' – hamster, tortoise and a tabby cat unimaginatively named Tiddles (I never knew an East End cat called anything else) who allowed me to dress him up in dolls' clothes. I also trained our hen, Ada, to pick up washing in her beak from the laundry basket for me to peg on to the clothes line and rescued many a tiny sparrow, setting them carefully into cardboard boxes lined with cotton wool. Human babies, however, held no more fascination for me than they did for my mum.

While other mothers cooed over babies in prams, mine sat with me in the Rex picture house in Roman Road market, sobbing over the death of Shep or Old Yeller. When my father returned from work one evening to find us yet again red-eyed with grief (this time over Bambi's mum), he insisted that enough was enough. From then on there would be only happy endings.

My mum, Margaret Mary Exley, always known as Margie, had had a tough childhood in London's East End. One of five children whose father, a docker, had died of TB as a young man, she had left school at four-teen to help support her family. To her, work was not only a question of economic necessity but the key to self-reliance. She had given birth to me at the age of thirty-three – unusually late, in the 1950s, for a woman to be having her first child – and a schoolfriend once commented to me how different she seemed from the other mums, most of whom had jobs in factories but dreamed of having enough money coming in to be able to stay at home with their children. My mum, on the other hand, had to be persuaded by my father to give up full-time employment to take care of me. She did so until I was four, but she couldn't wait to get back to work once I started infant school.

It was not as if she were a high-flying businesswoman with a fulfilling career. She worked as a waitress, on her feet all day, in a busy Kardomah coffee house on Kingsway in Holborn. But having known severe poverty growing up, she was in constant fear of sinking back into the kind of hand-to-mouth existence governed by pawnshops and tallymen. She seemed to live in a state of heightened reality, nerves strung taut, like a meerkat perpetually alert to danger. Yet at the same time she had a keen and tireless curiosity about other people, places and lifestyles that she could only glimpse in Hollywood films, and the coffee house, like the cinema, offered an escape from the daily grind of the East End. Every evening, she would come back with stale but exotic confections: sandwiches in rye bread, fruit croissants and Danish pastries – delicacies never found at that time among the custard tarts and pork pies of an East End bakery.

Many of her customers worked nearby at Bush House, the headquarters of the BBC World Service, and she would proudly bring home autographed photographs of 1960s 'celebrities' like the debonair newsreader Reggie Bosanquet, the actor Sam Kydd and even, rather surprisingly, strip-club owner Paul Raymond, the so-called 'King of Soho'.

Years later, one night in 1978, the television news was headlined by the mysterious death of the Bulgarian dissident novelist and playwright Georgi Markov, believed to have been murdered with the tip of a poisoned umbrella. My mother was distraught. Markov, who had worked for the BBC World Service since being granted political asylum in 1969, had been not only her customer but also her friend, chatting with her every day over coffee and always leaving a good tip. She knew him as 'my Georgie'. It's a wonder MI5 didn't take her in for background questioning.

My mother had been working at the Royal Mint at Tower Hill, swinging heavy bags of metal on to trucks, when she met my father, Bill Wassmer, a coiner who struck metal into money. Born in 1917, my dad was the eldest son of a soldier who had settled on Civvy Street as a baker. A dyed-in-the-wool trade union man, he was intelligent but for the most part self-educated. He became the long-term shop steward at the Mint, arguing his causes with considerable adversarial skill.

When they married in 1950 my parents put their names on the council housing list and moved into two upstairs rooms sublet to them by my father's uncle and aunt while they waited for a home of their own. In my mind's eye I can picture my father carrying their few possessions into their temporary accommodation at Lefevre Road whistling 'If I Knew You Were Comin' I'd've Baked a Cake', the cheery song popularised that year by Eileen Barton and Gracie Fields. Nearly twenty years later Jimi Hendrix and Led Zeppelin supplied a grittier soundtrack to the times – and my parents were still waiting to be rehoused.

They had already been at 25 Lefevre Road for three years when I came along on 5 January 1953, and there we would remain until 1969. The house was a Victorian terrace with a bay window flanked by tall pillars. In the 1950s and 1960s it was impossible to imagine that such decrepit slums would be sought after and gentrified by Thatcher's generation. They had leaking roofs and so much subsidence that the upper ceilings sagged alarmingly. Landlords never did repairs so, whenever there was heavy rain or snow, buckets had to be positioned at strategic points around the floors. We had a living room with a tiny kitchenette leading off it through an open doorway, one bedroom, an outside toilet and a rusting tin bath which hung on the garden wall – but no hot water. From time to time, mice scratched and scuttled in the wainscot. Occasionally they'd be sucked up by the Hoover, not a pleasant experience for us or for them. As I never had a bedroom of my own – I slept in the same room as my parents when I was small and graduated to the living-room sofa when I was older – I had no territory that was exclusively mine, no private place or space to keep my personal things, but as I knew nothing else I didn't feel deprived until I came to see how other people lived.

My parents were not so much a couple as two soulmates with their own individual interests – in my mother's case the pictures and her beloved Kardomah coffee house, and darts and the Hackney Wick dog track in my dad's. They were opposites, owl and fowl – she was a night person; he rose early. He was easygoing while she did most of the worrying. Television adverts warning of body odour or bad breath provoked paranoia in my mum since she had been born without a sense of smell. As a result she moved around in a cloud of cheap perfume, forever checking gas taps to make sure they weren't left on.

Although her education had been brief, my mother was bright and intuitive. An instinctive judge of character and situations, she seemed to understand what made people tick. She would instantly pick up on the importance of what remained unsaid in a conversation and at the Rex she always grasped the subtext of a film. My father often remarked that she was psychic. She certainly appeared to be able to read his mind and invariably knew exactly what he was about to say. Around him, she was never timid. Sensitive to the scars of her childhood privations, Dad had long ago assumed the role of her protector. Mum had been schooled by Irish nuns, and the Catholic guilt they instilled in her had been reinforced at home. After her father's early death, one of her elder brothers had taken on the role of the head of the family and when she was fourteen he had given her a good beating after catching her talking to a boy in the street. She never forgot the lesson acquired so painfully: we may be poor, but heaven help you if you bring shame on this family. Thereafter even bare arms were taboo. I can't recall her ever once wearing short sleeves, even during the occasional week we might spend at the Pontin's holiday camp in Pakefield, near Lowestoft.

My father, on the other hand, was a staunch Protestant and had no time for Catholicism. He was fond of making speeches about the need for clear, rational thought, unclouded by religious doctrine. It was impossible, he would say, for anyone to get a proper education at the hands of priests or nuns because they failed to teach children to think for themselves. He was a big fan of Oliver Cromwell, who stood against Charles I's assertion of the divine right of kings, and Martin Luther, who dared to rebel against the Pope.

At the age of four, safe from the clutches of priests and nuns, I started at the local infant school in Roman Road, opposite Kelly's eel and pie shop. I ate pie and mash, covered in the thick green parsley sauce known to East Enders as 'liquor', almost every lunchtime. Outside the shop, on the stall, slate-grey eels writhed in metal trays before being grabbed, chopped and stuffed into bags, the individual chunks still squirming as housewives carried them home to boil or steam.

Many of the children already knew each other from nursery. Being an only child as well as a newcomer, at first I was painfully shy. I was luckier than some of my classmates in that my mother had already taught me to read. In the afternoons our teacher would tell us stories and encourage us to tell our own, something in which we could all participate. I remember listening intently to one little girl's tale about a beautiful child called Ella who cleared the cinders from the grates for her ugly sisters. 'And so,' my classmate concluded triumphantly, 'they called her Cinder… Ella!' Oh, the wonderful logic of it! I was hooked.

'Does anyone else have a story for us?' asked the teacher.

In spite of my shyness, I felt my arm creep into the air almost involuntarily. I had a story to tell. I just hadn't thought it up yet.

Slowly and carefully, I constructed my contribution as I went along. My classmates co-operated kindly, listening with apparent fascination to a rambling tale about a tortoise. My love of storytelling had been born.

At home, I finished reading a whole book and was spellbound by it. It was the story of Joan of Arc. I related it to my dad, who was so impressed that when a man knocked on our door promising education for the price of a simple instalment plan, he immediately signed on the dotted line. And so *The Book of Knowledge* entered my life, a set of leather-bound encyclopaedias with gold embossed lettering on their spines.

As an only child I was already a kind of mini-adult, sandwiched somewhere between the two grown-ups I called Mum and Dad and their separate lives and passions. I amused myself by drawing pictures, writing stories and burying myself in *The Book of Knowledge*. Opening any one of the volumes could transform a dull, rainy afternoon. Hours sped by as new worlds sprang to life. I could learn about 'Our Giant Sun and its Gigantic Tasks', or take in 'The Story of Wheat'. In a section entitled 'The Mistress of the Adriatic', I read how Venetian prisoners would pass beneath the graceful Bridge of Sighs on their way to torture and death. Among photographic plates of amazing feats of engineering, or strange animals and insects like the Duck-Billed Platypus or the Bird-Eating Spider, were illustrated poems: 'From a Railway Carriage' by Robert Louis Stevenson I read aloud to myself, fascinated by its compelling steam-train tempo. Paintings featuring children, such as Velazquez's portrait of the Infanta Margaret Maria, were mesmerising even in black and white. A stunning drawing of a bespectacled Gulliver towing a captive fleet to Lilliput led me on to the public library, where a lender's card finally introduced me to a whole universe of characters and adventure. My head teeming with myriad stories drawn from Greek and Roman mythology, I allowed myself to dream: would I be as beautiful as the face that launched a thousand ships? As brave as Ajax? As wise as Minerva? I was venturing beyond the bounds of my childhood experience, and sometimes it could be scary. Was that a lorry that just passed, shaking our subsiding house, or the first rumblings of an earthquake like the one that destroyed Pompeii?

'The child's got too much imagination' was a comment I heard almost daily. It was meant to be a criticism but my father always took it as a compliment and continued the instalment-plan payments.

Great Uncle Will and Great Aunt Carrie, who lived downstairs, became my surrogate grandparents since my father and his own mother, Will's sister, Lil, were estranged. One Sunday afternoon, while I was still a baby, there had been an argument over the cooking of a joint of roast beef during which Lil had stormed out of our house, never to return. Both too proud to make the first move, my dad and his mother refused to contact one another and were never reconciled. We did once try to visit her, at my instigation: having no memory of my grandmother I was curious about her and questioned my father until he relented. It was a short trip – she lived in Stratford – but a long and tense journey for my dad. How would his mother receive him after not having laid eyes on him in almost ten years?

We knocked on the door and waited. In the end a neighbour came out and told us my grandmother wasn't in. It sounds bizarre, in these days of mobile phones and texts and round-the-clock communication, to pitch up on the doorstep of somebody you hadn't seen for years on the off chance she might be at home, but it wasn't so unusual then. We couldn't call ahead because we didn't have a phone. Maybe my grand-mother didn't have one, either, I don't know. But on that wet afternoon, as I watched my father's fingers nervously lighting damp cigarettes, I had a clear sense of his disappointment, though he never once gave voice to it. We simply turned round and went home. The visit was never attempted again. Feelings ran deep in my family – even about something as inconsequential as the cooking of roast beef.

So Aunt Carrie and Uncle Will Tolliday filled this family void. Described by all who knew them as 'characters', they were both frustrated entertainers. Carrie had a belting voice in the style of Gracie Fields and whatever Will lacked vocally he made up for with a terrifying and inventive act which involved an intricate and grotesque mask of rubber bands that covered every inch of his face. They would perform at the drop of a hat at various East End civic theatres, to patients trapped in hospital wards – any venue that would invite them.

The Bridge House, a little brown-tiled pub at the end of our street, was once treated to an impromptu show by Aunt Carrie while several of the notorious Kray twins' henchmen were trying to enjoy a quiet drink. After a few rounds of rum and blackcurrant, Carrie swept through the saloon bar singing 'It's a Sin to Tell a Lie' and swiped the glass from the impressive fist of a lantern-jawed villain. His eyes narrowed as she upbraided him in song in front of all the other customers. Finishing, bravely, on an astoundingly long note, she completed her performance by downing the man's drink. A hush descended on the bar. My mother leaned in quickly and whispered to him, 'She don't mean no harm. She's a relation of my husband's so if you can see your way to forgive, I'd be grateful.' She offered him her charming smile. After a slightly worrying pause, a low, rumbling chuckle could be heard. As it developed into a bellow of deep laughter everyone joined in. My mother had won him round.

At home Aunt Carrie and Uncle Will always had some creative project going on but they acted on strange whims, suddenly dyeing all their net curtains a shockingly bright canary yellow, for example, or painting each individual brick of our house a different colour. Carrie was also in the habit of pumping floral-scented fluid round her 'front rooms'. She minded me during the school holidays while my mother was at work and we would listen to *Mrs Dale's Diary* on the radio before sitting down to a lunch of tinned steak and kidney pudding, mashed potato and marrowfat peas. On long winter afternoons she would teach me complex card games like cribbage and solo. Resting by the crackling coal fire in the evenings she would weave romantic tales for me of how she and Uncle Will had met. I listened in wonder – until the object of her affections came home from the Bridge House with beer on his breath and a drunken domestic ensued, which rather ruined the magic.

In spite of their public ebullience, Will and Carrie were perturbed by any noise from upstairs – they were elderly, after all – and my parents, forever grateful to them for taking us in, bent over backwards to avoid annoying them in any way. The creaking of loose floorboards as we walked to and fro above their heads was a particular irritation so we all moved about on tiptoe, even my father, who was a heavy man and over six foot tall. Sometimes, to muffle the sound of my footsteps, my mother tied ribbon round my black plimsolls, encouraging me to imagine I was a ballerina. I would pretend to be Anna Pavlova dancing the Dying Swan, teetering lightly around the room *en pointe*.

When I started to make friends with other children at school it began to dawn on me not only that our domestic circumstances left something to be desired, but also that my family was, to say the least, a bit strange by other people's standards. Some of my classmates' parents had fared better than mine on the housing list and had already been moved into the new council tower blocks near Victoria Park. Their flats were luxuriously airy and light, yet warm in the winter – the kind of homes you might see on television adverts for gravy, where happy families sat smiling around the table as Mum, sporting a frilly pinny, served a slap-up meal in her spanking new Formica kitchen. Other friends lived in post-war prefabs, ramshackle but still standing, with wonderfully overgrown gardens.

What they all had that we didn't was space. They also had brothers and sisters, and the moment I was over their doorsteps my nostrils would be assailed not by something akin to the floral scents that permeated Aunt Carrie's 'front rooms' but by an unfamiliar cock-tail of stale milk, sweet vomit and the unsettling aroma of cloth nappies boiling in a saucepan. 'Hold my sister for me,' somebody would say, casually handing over a small alien creature. These girls were already trainee mums, tending confidently to their younger siblings, but I was terrified by the tiny, bawling infants that wriggled furiously in my awkward embrace, their faces scrunched into tight, red balls of discomfort.

Everyone else's parents appeared to have at least two children, and whether the adults had themselves grown up in happy or dysfunctional families, or in severe hardship like my mother, they all seemed to aspire to raising several kids, either to recreate a rosy childhood or to compensate for a rotten one. For a little girl whose ménage consisted of parents, assorted pets and the two oddballs who lived downstairs, it was something of an eye-opener.

Our extended family, on both my mother's and father's sides, was scattered, and with no phone and no car, it wasn't easy to stay in touch on a regular basis. Occasionally we would visit my father's sister, Aunt Joan, in Chigwell, but there were no big get-togethers with uncles, aunts and cousins all present. My dad's brother Lenny had died in the Second World War and his youngest sibling, Johnny, was nearly twenty years his junior. They seemed to have lost track of one another after my father's fall-out with his mum. As it was impossible for my parents to entertain relatives or friends in our cramped quarters at Lefevre Road, either we had to visit them or everyone went to the pub.

The exception was my mother's adored brother, another Johnny, a stevedore at the docks in Wapping. We often spent weekends with him and his wife Kath at their tenement flat at Riverside Mansions. While they drank with my parents in a pub by the Thames called the Jolly Sailor, I played outside with my five cousins, pacified with pennies and pop. We never crossed the threshold of the saloon bar, but from the street we would hear the drunken chatter subside from time to time when the jukebox played a sentimental tune or someone began to sing a heartbreaking Irish song about love and separation. 'I'm a Rover' was a favourite, and we kids would join in outside.

> ... *Though the night be dark as dungeon*
> *Not a star to be seen above*
> *I will be guided without stumble*
> *Into the arms of my only love.*

My father must have felt like an outsider among all the Catholic dock workers in the Jolly Sailor, and perhaps excluded by my mum's close relationship with her brother, too, but if he did, he kept it to himself.

After a raucous Saturday night, there would some-times be a church procession on Sunday. My younger cousin Catherine, dressed in lace like a baby doll, glided past Riverside Mansions one morning as though she had been set on a white raft sailing through the narrow docklands streets. I would be sent off to Mass with my cousins to stand mouthing an unfamiliar catechism while the priest came along flicking incense on us. Then, as if on cue, I would faint, sliding to the ground and regaining consciousness just in time to hear my cousins yet again blaming my father's religion. 'You're a Proddy dog. The incense found you out!' I don't think I'm the first person to suffer from fainting fits in church. It was probably due to low blood sugar or kneeling and standing up again too quickly, but there again, maybe my cousins were right.

One year we spent Christmas with Uncle Johnny and Aunt Kath – a real treat as Christmas at Lefevre Road was often fraught. There wasn't room for a proper tree so my mother would stand a small artificial one with silvery tinsel branches on the sideboard and painstakingly decorate it with lights and baubles. We had very few 13 amp sockets so the fairylights had to be plugged into the main light socket in the ceiling (all sorts of things had to be plugged into those sockets, including an electric blanket I had on my bed during the winter). My dad would come in from work and throw open the door. Being so tall, he would catch the wire and the whole lot would come crashing down. I have a memory of my mother once stamping on all the fallen baubles in frustration, crying, 'That's it! I give up!'

The flat at Riverside Mansions wasn't exactly pala-tial but there was a real sense of a family Christmas there, with presents hidden in every room to be hunted for in a clamour early in the morning. In material terms my cousins were poorer than I was, but they had some-thing I didn't: each other. I shared a bed with my cousins Pat and Catherine. On the night before Christ-mas, as I lay there between them, still wide awake, Pat, sensing that I was fretful, took me in her arms and cuddled me. For the first time I was acutely aware that, as an only child, I was missing out on a sense being part of a loving clan of children. My cousins might have scrapped like cats and dogs but they would support each other through good times and bad.

There were other cousins I got to see less frequently because their parents had settled in Essex, part of the diaspora from the East End tempted either by the promise of work at the Ford car factory or by the offer of a brand-new council house. My father was always disparaging about Essex. The new housing estates there were, he said, 'ersatz' and he dismissed Dagenham as 'Corned Beef City'. Looking back, these estates were rather sterile and soulless. The residents became overly houseproud and couldn't help being sucked into a culture of keeping up with the Joneses. Front lawns were fastidiously manicured, cars washed even when they were already clean and curtains twitched in streets where very little happened. To an East End kid, a Sunday afternoon in Essex was depressingly quiet. In Becontree or Chigwell even the lone bell of an ice-cream van, isolated as it was from the accompanying sights and sounds of Sunday activities at home – the bustle of Brick Lane market, drunks singing in the pubs, radio broadcasts wafting from open windows – struck a mournful note. In spite of our less than ideal living conditions, my parents much preferred the rough and tumble of East London and would never have entertained the notion of moving away. For all its shortcomings, it was home.

Chapter Two

The Number 8 Bus

M y dad cycled to work every morning and, as a small child, I was sometimes allowed to go with him, propped on the crossbar of his bike. He would weave his way through the City traffic and, as we approached Tower Hill, the Mint would suddenly appear, more imposing even than Buckingham Palace. On entering the building we followed long corridors whose high ceilings were studded with chandeliers, my father pausing to speak to important-looking men in rooms where plush, draped curtains swirled on polished floors. I wandered around, looking up at fine old paintings on the walls as they talked of 'bonuses', 'incentives' and 'demarcation'. Then I would descend with my father to the furnace room, where 'his men' were waiting for him. After the graciously appointed upper offices, it was a vision of hell.

As soon as the door to this inferno opened I was hit by a blast of searing heat. At first, dazzled by the light, I could make out no more than the black silhouettes of men heaving long-handled pans of molten metal. As my eyes adjusted the smiling faces of my father's colleagues would come into focus: they always made a huge fuss of me because I was 'Bill Wassmer's kid'. Boiled sweets or spearmint gum would be pressed upon me while locker doors were hastily and courteously closed on the busty pin-ups glued alongside photos of Billy Fury or Elvis.

The men looked up to my father because he was their shop steward. Before long they would have even greater reason to respect him: he was soon to engage in what would turn out to be a long drawn-out battle over plans to relocate the Royal Mint to Wales. It was a mission that was to preoccupy him for the rest of his life and in the process he would cross swords with three chancellors of the exchequer.

When I was seven I moved up to the local primary school, which was named after the great Labour MP and former leader of the party, George Lansbury, who had been a prominent campaigner for social justice and improved living and working conditions in the East End. My father thought that entirely appropriate for a good shop steward's kid. I was too big by this time to ride to the Mint on his crossbar, but old enough, he decided, to be introduced to some of his other interests. A keen sportsman, my dad had been an amateur boxer as a young man and taught me how to spar when I was only six or seven. I was, he informed me as I ducked and weaved in the garden, 'a southpaw'. Before I was born he had travelled around the country, accompanied by my mother, to compete in darts tournaments. In our cluttered living room an elegant grandfather clock stood trapped behind an armchair. Only part of the inscription was visible: 'Bill Wassmer – Champion…'. The rest of it didn't matter. That was all a little girl needed to know about her dad.

Although we took care not to disturb Will and Carrie by treading too heavily on the floorboards, behind the closed doors of our flat it was never quiet. My mother couldn't tolerate silence, especially at night. It was like death to her. Consequently clocks ticked perpetually in the bedroom and sitting room, and whenever one of them stopped, it would be wound up instantly, as if it were a heartbeat needing to be restarted. All through the daylight hours, either the radio would be blaring or LPs would be spinning on a turntable, playing soulful ballads by Ray Charles or Frank Ifield. I learned to switch off from my surroundings while reading or writing my stories. On Sundays, however, we listened to comedy radio programmes together, *The Navy Lark* or *Round the Horne*. I laughed along with my parents, though the double entendres went over my head. I was just happy that they were happy. If I could make them laugh myself, I thought, what a great thing that would be.

All children are eager to please but, looking back, there was an extra dimension to my desire to make my parents smile. My mother's permanent anxiety had instilled in me, if only on a subconscious level, a desire to 'protect' her. So I avoided doing or telling her anything that might upset her and instead began to try to amuse her. I developed a repertoire, performing passable impressions for my parents of the eccentric upper-crust actress Margaret Rutherford, or Ethel Merman giving her all to 'There's No Business Like Show Business'.

Downstairs in one of Aunt Carrie's front rooms there was a piano. I couldn't read music, but with the easier pieces it was hardly rocket science working out which note on the sheet music corresponded to which piano key, and I taught myself to play 'Für Elise'.

'D'you hear that? Beethoven! The child's a genius!' cried my family.

I accepted all attention and applause gratefully, a slightly precocious little girl seeking her place in a household of adults.

I might have been presenting a façade of maturity, but while I perceived problems in the way an adult would, I didn't yet have the emotional resources to deal with them. Left to my own devices much of the time, I relied on my thought processes rather than on emotions to find solutions. By now I realised that my family wasn't different. There was always an unspoken acknowledgement between my father and me that my mother was 'sensitive'. I may have wondered whether she was the one who needed taking care of, but these matters were never discussed by any of us. So I laughed and clowned, wanting no more than for my mother to be happy and my dad to be proud of me.

I can see now how this atmosphere of denial, of avoiding difficult issues, influenced most of the decisions I took throughout their lives, and certainly the biggest I ever made in mine.

I wasn't the only one keeping secrets. I can't have been more than about seven when, at a loose end on a Sunday afternoon, I started poking about in our bedroom. With my parents' double bed and my single one shoehorned into such a small space, the room was crammed with furniture. An old utility dressing table was wedged behind my bed and though it was almost impossible to open its drawers completely my small hands could reach right inside them. There I found a stash of interesting papers: my birth certificate, a black-edged death certificate for an Irish grandmother I had never met and my parents' wedding certificate, on which my father was described as 'bachelor'. Next to my mother's name was an entry I could read but did not understand. She was described as 'the divorced wife of George Townsend'.

Later that evening, while my parents were watching television, I broached the subject of my discovery. 'What does "the divorced wife of George Townsend" mean?'

They exchanged glances.

'It's a mistake,' said my father. 'The man who wrote the certificate got things wrong.'

I sensed this wasn't the whole story. Over the years I would ask them again and again about the wedding certificate. I knew from the awkward looks they always gave one another that they were hiding something. I would be grown up and my father would be dead before I finally got the truth out of my mother.

The constant need to ensure they did nothing that might give rise to complaints made domestic life very stressful for my parents. Any storm in a teacup could mean the difference between keeping our leaking roof over our heads and being thrown out on to the street. An incident that occurred when I was eight brought home to me just how potent was their fear of being made homeless. The man next door had a large pigeon coop in his garden and lost a fair number of his birds to the neighbourhood cats. One day he decided enough was enough and erected a high fence of timber-framed chicken wire on top of the existing one, extending its height to ten or twelve feet. It surrounded the entire garden – including the sloping roof of the outside toilet beneath the upstairs kitchen window – giving it the appearance of an incongruously sited tennis court.

Carrie and Will, always prone to peculiar home improvements and evidently taken by the idea, chose to follow suit. Almost overnight more chicken-wire fencing went up, blocking Tiddles' route from our kitchen window to the garden. Negotiations immediately began on the cat's behalf, with my father calling upon his considerable negotiating skills to try to reach an agreement with Carrie and Will while my mother used all her charm on our neighbour. Neither side would budge. They were all determined that their gardens would remain cat-free zones.

Tiddles suffered, scratching and mewing to go out and trying without success to find a way through the impossibly high fence from the sloping roof of our outside loo. He fretted and caterwauled and soiled both the rooms in which we lived. My animal-loving mother simply couldn't comprehend how anyone, let alone members of our own family, could do this to our pet. In the end it fell to my father to solve the problem.

A week later, I learned that my dad had secured a new home for Tiddles with a kind elderly lady on a country farm. There he could spend the remainder of his days with all the space in the world to roam. I was heartbroken to be losing him but I had witnessed his appalling distress and understood there was no other way. My mother put on a brave face but her eyes were red on the morning of his departure. We owned no cat basket for his journey so my dad had decided to improvise with a holdall. Tiddles took one look at it and disappeared under the sofa. I tempted my old tom cat out far enough to grab him by the scruff of his burly neck and stuff him into the bag. He struggled as I zipped it up. My parents looked on as I told Tiddles firmly it was for his own good. Suddenly the cat was quiet. My father took the holdall and quickly left the house. Immediately the front door clicked shut behind him my mother burst into tears, confirming the fear that had been growing in my mind all morning.

'He's not going to a farm, is he?'

My mum shook her head. 'Your dad's taking him to be put down because people don't want him in their gardens,' she said bitterly.

She began to sob and I joined in, wracked with guilt over the part I had played in sending Tiddles to his death. So much for happy endings.

After that, my mother refused ever again to speak to the man next door, which was hardly fair since Tiddles's fate had in truth been sealed by Carrie and Will. But because of our dependence on their goodwill, she was never able to confront them over the matter. It was another reminder of how little control my parents exercised over their own lives. My mum's hope was that, one day, the council would eventually rehouse us, she would have some autonomy over her own household and I would have a room to myself. But it became increasingly apparent that we were low priority as far as the council was concerned. I was the only child in the family so, theoretically at least, we were not overcrowded. Until our turn came the only escape for my parents was work by day and the pub or racetrack by night.

I regularly went dog racing with my dad but my mother rarely joined us. Perhaps she was secretly jealous of my father's passion, since even on their wedding day, she claimed, he had deserted her at the pub reception to catch the last few races at the Wick.

As a small child at the track I would be surrounded by men standing on tiptoe, jostling, pushing and jabbing rolled-up racecards in the air, all eyes fixed on six greyhounds tearing round a wide circuit after an electric hare.

'Gertcha, four!'

'Get out there, six!'

My father would put his strong arm around me, sheltering me from the shoving men but, just like theirs, his gaze would be on the finishing line as he willed his dog towards it. Racing greyhounds had names like Mick the Miller, Prairie Peg or Pigalle Wonder. No Rovers or Fidos here. I would look up at my father, seeing how tall he rose above the other men – a giant with thick, grey, curly hair.

The second the race ended I would know from the expression on his face whether he had won or lost; whether he was crushed, excited or simply relieved to have held on to some of his money with a place bet. He would tell me the numbers of the winning dogs so that I could check the hundreds of discarded betting slips on the ground to make sure none of them had been thrown away by mistake. I never once came across a winning ticket but it kept me busy while he made his next selection. I would find him at the Tote, asking a lady behind a metal grille for 'six to win' then 'four and six about'. Greyhound betting was complicated, perhaps even to some adults: there were forecast bets, reverse forecasts, quinellas, triellas and accumulators; bets on 'win' dogs or dogs to come first or second or in either order.

My father would take his tickets, put them carefully in his pocket, engulf my small hand in his and sweep me along to the bookies near the track. They stood on boxes, chalking and re-chalking the changing odds on their blackboards, all the while keeping an eagle eye on the Gladstone bags full of cash at their feet. Once my dad had studied the dogs in the enclosure I was allowed to choose one. I knew that head down and tail between the legs were good signs. If we won, we'd make for the track caff for a celebration supper. The latest thing was Russian salad, which consisted of tinned mixed vegetables in warm salad cream. My father was in his element. This was his favourite place in all the world.

My mum found a different way to relax. After a hard shift at the coffee house she would come home and do the housework, tidying, cleaning and trying to find somewhere to store everything. Clothes went into the sideboard and my school socks hung over dinner plates in a rack on the cooker. It must have been so demoralising for her. When she had finished she would light up her first Rothmans cigarette of the day, her hand trembling uncontrollably until all the stress began to drain out of her. Then she would get herself ready for a night out at the Bridge House: hair teased, combed and lacquered to within an inch of its life, cheekbones rouged, nose powdered, lips painted, comfortable work shoes replaced by stiletto heels. A black patent handbag filled with make-up and tissues and a coat with a real fur collar completed the look. I marvelled at the transformation – to me she was more beautiful than the star of any movie.

Sometimes we would all go to the Bridge House, where the landlady would allow me to sit on a stool behind the bar with Sandy, the pub dog, perched on my lap. I dipped cheese and onion crisps into glasses of Britvic tomato juice, watching the customers lose their inhibitions along with their sobriety, breaking into song, tears or laughter as the mood took them. At other times, my mother, the night owl, went alone. It was only a five-minute walk but one that involved passing the coal merchant's dark and menacing forecourt. Late at night, I'd listen for the familiar footsteps, the sound of her heels clicking on the pavement outside, sometimes with a tipsy trip, signalling that all was well.

My world then was bounded by a handful of landmarks: school, the dog track, the pub and the Rex picture house. But somewhere out there, past Spitalfields and the City, was the West End, where my mother took me twice a year to have my hair cut by the children's hairdresser at Selfridges. 'Curly cut,' she would instruct. 'Parting on the left.' I would sit in the elegant salon watching the snowy-white muslin curtains at the windows waft gracefully in the breeze. Afterwards came the scent of eau-de-Cologne as gentle fingers massaged my scalp. Looking back, it's hard for me to fathom why my mum chose to splash out on such a treat for me, let alone how she could have afforded it on her wages. Perhaps she just wanted one luxury for her child. Perhaps, for half an hour twice a year, it was a treat for her, too, to allow herself to imagine she shared the lifestyle of people who had their hair cut at Selfridges as a matter of course.

Apart from such outings, the West End remained as much of a mystery to me as Venice and the Bridge of Sighs in *The Book of Knowledge*. Then, one evening at dusk, I saw Great Uncle Will striding down our street dressed in a stunning military-style costume: epaulettes perched on each shoulder, gold braiding across his chest. I thought he must have joined the cavalry. The real source of this splendid uniform turned out to be even more glamorous. He had been for a job interview and was now a newly appointed commissionaire at the London Palladium. Off he would go each evening, returning in the early hours of the morning with tales of having opened a door for Frank Sinatra or Marlene Dietrich. I realised now that the West End was within reach. Somewhere at the top of the road, a number 8 bus could take you out of the East End and into a wonderful world full of stars and endless possibilities.

Chapter Three

By Hope, By Work, By Faith

I am nine years old and my teacher at George Lansbury primary school is a woman called Joyce LeWars. She is from Jamaica and walks with her head held high, proud, strutting – her body so curvy it seems to have been drawn from a series of circles. I creep up behind her when she's climbing stairs and hear her humming a strange but cheerful tune. I wish I could join in. She's the happiest person I know.

Before Mrs LeWars, primary school had been a strict and forbidding place revolving around the three Rs and the slipper. Our teachers had all been middle-aged men in tweed jackets, and women who wore milk-bottle-bottom glasses. And before Mrs LeWars, I had only seen one other black person in my life: a tall stranger wearing a Homburg hat and white suit, baggy trousers flapping wide in the breeze as he strode through Roman Road market. No one knew where he had come from or where he was going, but all heads had turned – adults fearful, children fascinated.

Mrs LeWars inspired the same fascination. She managed her class with just the right mixture of authority and praise and was everyone's mum, encouraging us all in equal measure. We spent long, hot summer afternoons writing essays and stories which she would take home for her own five children to read. They joined us one summer at a school camp in the countryside – two dozen East End kids suddenly transplanted to rural Surrey to tramp around potteries and old churches. More accustomed to playing in the wartime bombsites that still existed in London in the early 1960s, we now found ourselves let loose on a more natural landscape. We screamed as we galloped like runaway horses down the Devil's Punchbowl – an impressively deep, dry valley sculpted by water long ago, we were told. The next day someone complained of a sore throat, brought on not by screaming, it was discovered, but by a raging virus. Those who didn't end up in sick bay took it home with them and suffered there.

Still, we also took home memories of a new experience. It was 1963 and our lives seemed to be changing as though the planet itself was turning in a different way. From the dodgem cars and waltzers in the fairground at Victoria Park a new music was sounding. It, too, had a different beat – created not by lush orchestral strings but picked out on guitars and rough harmonicas

– a Mersey beat. In the wider world that year was notable for a series of salacious scandals, including the sensational divorce of the Duke and Duchess of Argyll. Every evening during the television news I would hear my parents complaining in hushed tones about upper-class depravity or ministerial falls from grace. Something called 'the Profumo affair' was on everyone's lips. John Profumo, a respected Tory cabinet minister with a film-star wife, had been forced to resign after being caught in a web of intrigue involving call-girls and a Russian spy. The details went over my head but there seemed to be a general feeling in the air that the establishment was rocking on its heels and an old, hidebound way of life was being overturned.

At school a new wave of forward-thinking and politically motivated teachers had been spearheaded by the arrival of a young, innovative headmaster, Mr Kent, who, at the end of that year, led a special assembly to mourn the death of American President Kennedy, giving a memorable speech celebrating democracy and equality.

Soon another member of staff appeared, wearing long hair and a black PVC raincoat. Mr Rogers had been trained at the Central School of Speech and Drama and had come to teach us 'acting'. With him came a lot of big wooden boxes, open on one side, which could be fitted together in various combinations of shape and size to form a stage. Instead of whacking us with a slipper, he prompted us to explore it. We

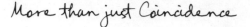

leaped on to it, pretending to be all manner of things
– trees, birds, angry, sorry, sad.

One afternoon Mr Rogers took four of us to one side
and introduced us to Shakespeare. Christine Bolton, Pat
Pask, Sharon Warren and I were then ten years old, but
after a few weeks' coaching we were also word-perfect
for the Witches' scenes in *Macbeth*. A month later we
were confidently applying panstick make-up, cloaks,
wigs and talons and stepping out on to the stage at
Aldgate's Toynbee Theatre, waiting for the curtains to
open and the lights to go up.

John Profumo, the disgraced government minister,
was atoning for his sins by cleaning toilets in the same
building. Perhaps he even watched the Shakespeare
Festival in which we played our parts.

Double, double toil and trouble; fire burn, and caul-
dron bubble…

As Hecate I had a thirty-five line speech but after Mr
Rogers's expert coaching, I didn't forget a word. The
rest of our class, together with proud teachers and
parents, boomed applause from the stalls.

On the Central Line train home to Mile End, my
father looked on as my classmates carried my broom-
stick for me. He smiled across at me, full of pride,
having had no idea we had even been rehearsing, let
alone would be performing in a proper theatre. A few
weeks later, coming home with my dad from the Bridge
House one evening, my mother flung her patent leather
handbag on the sofa.

'Do you have to keep going on?' she snapped. 'People go out for a quiet drink – they don't want to keep hearing about "my kid this and my kid that".'

My father had been bragging again, boring pub regulars not just with his account of the theatre production but with news that I had now passed the Eleven-Plus, one of only two girls in my class to do so.

This was the exam that would separate me from the friends I had grown up with, scattering us in different directions. After the summer holidays I would be moving on to the Central Foundation School for Girls in Spital Square, on the edge of the City. My friends would be attending secondary moderns where, in 1964, academic subjects were superseded by lessons designed to prepare them for the kind of life it was assumed working-class girls would go on to lead. If they showed the aptitude for it, they learned shorthand and typing. If not, they had classes in something called 'layette'. I hadn't the faintest idea what this was – it sounded to me like the name of some French perfume – until it was explained to me that it was guidance for what to buy and make for your baby. Girls as young as fifteen years old filled exercise books with notes on essential babycare items and were instructed how to knit and sew everything from baby blankets to burp cloths.

The boys, too, were set on diverging paths. Those who passed the Eleven-Plus would go on to a new local grammar school while those who failed might learn woodwork at a secondary modern or technical college.

After term ended, my friends and I took a trip on the number 8 bus to the West End. With pocket money given to me by my dad, I paid for us to see *Zulu*, with Michael Caine, on a huge cinema screen in Piccadilly. Afterwards, we headed to Trafalgar Square where we fed the pigeons, took farewell photos of one other and tried to make sense of the message Mr Rogers had written in each of our autograph books: 'Keep to the Coven'.

Although we promised to stay in touch, deep down we all knew, even then, that it wasn't going to happen. We went home on the bus together and after we'd said our goodbyes I lingered a moment at the bus stop, knowing I'd be returning to it soon. I would be taking the number 8 out of the East End every day to my new school, while my friends remained behind. But riding with me would be my father's expectations. Could I possibly ever live up to them?

On the heels of my Eleven-Plus result had come news of another exam I'd sat. I had passed that one, too, and if my father was pleased as Punch that I had gained a place at a grammar school, this was the icing on the cake. I had been awarded a bursary that would fund my school uniform until the day I left. The Alleyn Award hadn't been won for years, but I'd done it.

When the bursary came through my mum and I travelled up to the City to buy my uniform, which could only be purchased from Gamage's department store at 116–128 Holborn. Once known as the people's popular emporium, Gamage's no longer exists – it closed its doors in the 1970s – but at one time it had been among London's best-known stores. It had sold everything from picnic baskets to magic tricks to motoring accessories, as well as boasting an international shipping service that had, in its glory days, dispatched goods 'throughout the empire'. Much loved by small boys for its seemingly endless array of model trains, aeroplanes, bicycles and 'scholar's microscopes', it had become the official supplier of uniforms to the Boy Scout movement. In 1964, it also stocked every item on the exhaustive list we had received from the Central Foundation School for Girls, or CFS, as it was known.

In the girlswear department, a smart, well-spoken lady hurried across to attend to us. I sensed my mother's unease. Perhaps she would have been happier if the tables had been turned and she had been serving this woman a cup of coffee in her Kardomah overall. She reacted by adopting a new voice for the afternoon, one more fitting to her new station as respected customer.

We handed our list to the assistant, who led us to various rails and stacked shelves, selecting bottle-green gymslips and skirts, green-and-red-striped ties, gingham summer dresses, starched white shirts and sports gear suitable for hockey and something called lacrosse. I stepped out of changing cubicles looking, and feeling, uncomfortable in stiff-collared blouses. My mother checked the price of each item. It was all shockingly expensive. Stunned by the mounting subtotal, she started to panic, insisting on large sizes I could grow into, until the sales assistant reminded her as tactfully as she could that since the bursary paid for a full six years there was no need to economise. I heaved a sigh of relief. I had no intention of starting a new school swamped in voluminous skirts when the mini was all the rage.

We stepped out into sunshine, laden with bags. The Kardomah coffee house was only a few bus stops along the road and my mum couldn't resist dropping in so the Saturday waitresses could see where we had been. 'Julie's grammar school uniform,' she said proudly, raising a Gamage's bag.

There was more to be done when we got the uniform home. Every item had to have its own name tag. My mother considered the instruction ruefully, then went out to the market and bought iron-on labels. Life was too short for a working woman to sew.

Seven years before, the prime minister, Harold Macmillan, had told us all we 'had never had it so good', but in the East End, at least, we were only just beginning to agree with him. By 1964, 'Live now, pay later' was the slogan of the day. No one seemed to fear hire-purchase agreements any more and labour-saving goods were at the top of every shopping list. My mother now flicked through catalogues to make her purchases. Tupperware was the latest thing, and she invested in lunchboxes and drinks containers that I could take with me to school. At long last we got our first fridge, powered by gas, and the milk came in from its saucepan of cold water on the window ledge. While I experimented with fruit-cordial ice cubes my mum, who had never been much of a one for shopping or cooking and had at last been emancipated by a three-star ice compartment, embraced the new frozen-food options with enthusiasm. Out went the old staples of corned beef, spam and tinned ravioli and in came exotic convenience meals like fish fingers and crinkle-cut chips.

The flat itself, though, was deteriorating further. The roof had sprung more leaks, a paisley patch of damp was spreading out across the bedroom ceiling and there was even more subsidence in the living room. Uncle Will had brought home a cute mongrel puppy he christened Judy and in the summer holidays I escaped most days to walk her in Victoria Park and teach her tricks. Or I would go to the local Odeon for an hour or so to be whisked off to considerably more glamorous locations a galaxy away from Mile End: Istanbul in the to-catch-a-thief caper *Topkapi*, or the beautiful American mansion, with its stables and horses, to which handsome Sean Connery brings ice-cool Tippi Hedren in Hitchcock's *Marnie*.

At home I shut myself off from whatever was going on around me and worked on my Olivetti typewriter, which my mother had bought me for my birthday six months earlier. It came with a smart grey case containing a neat pouch where I could store pens, paper and envelopes. I loved every task associated with it, no matter how small – changing the ribbon, feeding in the paper, snapping down the bar to keep it in place – just like those men who are never happier than when they are tinkering with their cars. When I was ready I would position my hands above the keys like a concert pianist before allowing my two forefingers to dance across them, impressing on the paper poems and stories set in places I had only ever read about or seen at the cinema: Mediterranean islands like Rhodes, home to the Colossus, and beautiful Capri, where the emperor Tiberius had thrown his enemies off a high cliff.

By the autumn the Macmillan government, still reeling from the Profumo affair, was listing as badly as 25 Lefevre Road. My father was now confident that a Labour prime minister would soon be in power and the class barriers would come crashing down.

The seeds of such a revolution had already been sown. In what seemed like a strange reversal of the natural order, Terence Stamp, Michael Caine, the Beatles and Peter Sellers, working-class heroes all, were mixing with the likes of Princess Margaret and Lord Snowdon. London in the 1960s has been described as the place where our modern world began and we were seeing the emergence of a new meritocracy, where talent mattered more than who your parents were. One of its first stars was the photographer David Bailey, born in Leytonstone, while the East End's own Vidal Sassoon, who had given the fashion supremo Mary Quant her iconic bob cut, was famous all over the world.

Throughout the summer a pristine satchel has been sitting permanently by the door, filled with blank note-books: the unwritten story of my career at the Central Foundation School for Girls. On 14 September 1964 I put on my new uniform, slip the strap of the satchel across my shoulder and set off for the bus stop.

The stiff white blouse puffs up out of the loose waistband of my skirt as I raise my arm to hail the number 8. Unsure how I should wear my beret, I've tried it several ways: at jaunty French angles, like a workman's cap and, lastly, drawn down at the back like a snood. I catch sight of my reflection in the bus window as I jump on board. The beret looks like a flat, green dinner plate perched on my head. Climbing the stairs to the upper deck, I spot an empty seat but before I can reach it I am pounced upon by a swarm of older girls, all wearing the same bottle-green uniform as mine.

Panicked, I fall to the floor and a scuffle breaks out. I'm kicking and struggling but someone grabs my beret and when I eventually manage to break free it is tossed back at me. I see that its stalk is missing.

'You've been bobbled!' they scream, clattering down the stairs, cackling.

A third of the pupils at my new school are Jewish, most of whom live in Stepney and Whitechapel. Many are from families that fled Poland and Germany in the late 1930s and 1940s and have relatives who survived concentration camps. They have dark hair and strange names like Bobravitch and Baruch. The only two 'foreigners' I have ever known before are Mrs LeWars and a boy called Remo Randolfi whose family run a café and ice-cream parlour in Roman Road. Now I am about to become 'foreign' myself, albeit only for half an hour, when I am wrongly seated on the kosher lunch table, perhaps because I, too, am dark-haired and have an odd surname.

Years later I would discover that my roots are a mixture of French Jewish and Irish Catholic, but on my first day at senior school, I was happy to be whatever they wanted me to be.

The CFS had stood in Spital Square since 1890, but dated back to a much earlier era. It had been endowed as a free charity school for boys and girls in 1726, but had very probably existed as a parochial charity school since 1702. The Edwardian red-brick building was bordered on one side by Spitalfields fruit market, where I had to pick my way through squashed, sometimes rotten fruit to reach the gates. Often I would come across hard-up East Enders or refugees sorting through it to rescue the more edible specimens. On the other side was Bishopsgate, gateway to the City, its banks and its money, and a couple of miles further on, the West End.

This location, at the midway point between East End and West End, seemed an apt metaphor for how I would come to see myself in my grammar school years: suspended in a no-man's-land between a past I was being educated out of and a future still beyond my reach.

At primary school I had benefited from a progressive approach that treated education as a springboard to social mobility and mirrored the changing times. Walking through the door of the CFS, by contrast, was like stepping into the past. The grammar school (motto: *Spe Labore Fide* – by hope, by work, by faith) clung resolutely to its traditions and its illustrious history. Instead of drama there was elocution, long afternoons spent trying to recite Keats' odes without giving yourself away with the merest suggestion of a flattened Cockney vowel. Latin mistresses led us through the tedious declension of nouns. The only hint of the Swinging Sixties was the occasional polka-dot mini-skirt a brave young supply teacher might dare to wear. Our headmistress, the jealous guardian of the school's antiquated standards and customs, was apparently unaware of any smashing down of class barriers. Her pride and joy was the board that hung outside her office displaying, in gold lettering, the names of all the girls who had gone on to Oxbridge. Katharine Whitehorn's later description of tradition as 'habit in a party frock' would have found no resonance here.

In truth the school was already an anachronism by the time I entered its hallowed portals. The expansion of the comprehensive system, where state schools did

not select their pupils on the basis of academic achievement, was already underway and the election of a
Labour government the very next month escalated the
demise of the grammar school in all but a handful of
areas of the country. The Central Foundation School
was duly obliged to go comprehensive and in 1975
would relocate to new premises in Bow.

In my first year I worked hard and came top of the
class in nearly all subjects. Subsequent years were a
different matter, however, as it became increasingly
evident that I'd been hot-housed by my trendy primary
school and then dumped in an institutional backwater.
It was *Goodbye Mr Chips* minus the charismatic teacher.
The school refused to acknowledge that I was finding
certain subjects difficult: in their eyes, I was simply not
trying hard enough. I had been put into the top stream
to work towards O-Level maths, for example, but when
the lessons became more advanced and I began to lag
behind they refused to allow me to drop down into the
CSE stream. If they had done so, I might have coped
better. It would also have given me the opportunity to
study other subjects for which I showed more flair and
interest, such as music. It was as though the school was
determined I should not be permitted to benefit from
my lack of effort, even though the reason behind it was
a lack of aptitude.

My dad still bragged at the Bridge House about his
clever kid but the only subjects in which I maintained
good grades were English, foreign languages and

history. In other lessons I acted the clown, entertaining my classmates with my updated repertoire of impressions, which now included Cilla Black and Sandie Shaw. My school reports showed how badly I was trailing in maths and sciences and my father was frustrated. I had lost interest in school but he made excuses for me, knowing it was difficult for me to concentrate on homework without a room of my own.

Concerns about my academic performance took a back seat when Uncle Johnny became ill. He had suffered health problems ever since the war, during which he'd served in the Royal Army Medical Corps, attached to The West African Frontier Force. He had been injured during the D-Day landings and my mother often spoke of how he had arrived home in a pitiful condition, stricken by dysentery. Now when we visited Riverside Mansions there were no afternoons spent singing in the Jolly Sailor. My cousins and I were told to keep quiet: their father had terminal cancer. Uncle Johnny struggled up and down the stairs, yellow with jaundice, his face contorted by pain. At the end of the war his unit had also helped to liberate Belsen; now, in the last days of his life, he looked like one of its victims. When he finally died, my mother collapsed.

Shortly after the cremation, she went off one evening to the Bridge House with my father. She returned drunk, in distress and arguing with him. My dad told her to pull herself together and accept that Uncle Johnny was gone but she continued to rail at him.

Swaying in the tiny kitchenette, she stumbled, fell under the table and lay there crying out in pain like a wounded animal. I had never seen anyone so bereft and tried to help her to her feet but it was impossible. Although she was slightly built she was a dead weight, heavy with sorrow and alcohol. I looked to my father but, still smarting from their row, and possibly trying to allay my anxiety, he seemed uncharacteristically cold and distant. 'Just leave her where she is,' he ordered. I hesitated, unsure of what to do.

As he walked through to the living room, my mother suddenly gathered her strength and chose a target for her rage and grief. 'I wish it had been you instead of him!' she screamed.

I didn't need to see my father's face to know what a terrible thing she had just said. She knew it too. Still slumped under the table, she began to wail. My loyalties were torn. I was a kid. What was I to do? I stood up and made a decision. I did what my father had told me to do. I left my mother on the kitchen floor to cry herself to sleep. In the morning she got ready and went off to work without uttering a word about what had happened the night before.

That incident was shocking, not least because it was never mentioned. If I had always been aware of my mother's fragility, now I had seen her behaving more like a child than a parent. Worse, my father, her steadfast protector, had turned his back on her that night, and I had abandoned her, too. Perhaps I had realised that I couldn't be her mother, and she couldn't absolutely be mine. If I had always instinctively avoided rocking the boat at home, from that moment on I made a conscious effort to ensure she was never upset.

I had come to understand something significant: in general grown-ups might be able to sweep away problems and fears, but in my family it was probably best to keep unpalatable truths, and your feelings, to yourself.

Chapter Four

Rebel Without a Cause

On a summer's afternoon I am sitting in a French lesson singing, along with my classmates, a French song about a shepherdess.

Il était une bergère
et ron ron ron petit patapon
Il était une bergère
qui gardait ses moutons, ron ron
qui gardait ses moutons.

Unable to concentrate in the heat, and because of a dragging pain low in my belly, I keep forgetting the words. I feel wretched, uncomfortable and out of sorts, and beads of sweat are breaking out on my forehead. At last the bell rings and as I get to my feet I know instantly that something isn't right. I make for the toilets.

I have just started my first period. Emerging from the cubicle to wash my hands and splash my face with water, I glance up at my reflection in the mirror. I still look the same, even though I am now supposed to be a 'woman'.

Later, at home, I stole two sanitary towels from the drawer where I knew my mother hid them. No slender, adhesive-backed pads in endless shapes and sizes for the 1960s woman: just bulky towels with loops at each end that had to be attached to a special belt. And I didn't have a belt. When my mum came home from work I felt unable to tell her what had happened. I couldn't help feeling I had done something wrong. Perhaps I had. I was growing up.

When I was nine my mother had taken me to our family doctor, concerned about the swellings beneath my nipples. I had taken off my T-shirt while Dr Teverson gently felt my tiny breasts, his eyes decorously closed behind his heavy horn-rimmed spectacles. My mother looked on anxiously. Finally the doctor gave his verdict: puberty, pure and simple. My mother protested. At nine years old? How could a child so young display the seeds of womanhood when she herself had been flat-chested until she gave birth to me? Dr Teverson tried to reassure her – girls developed earlier these days, he said – but if my mother was reassured, she wasn't convinced, and she had never once broached the subject of menstruation with me. I had to find out about that at school.

In some ways I was relieved we hadn't talked about it since that appointment at the doctor's surgery had instilled a sense of unease, if not guilt, about the way my body had begun to change. Other girls of twelve had flat chests but still proudly wore 'teen bras'. I envied them as I ran around hockey fields and netball pitches with only a tight vest to restrain my bouncing bosom. My mother seemed to have a blind spot as far as my physical development was concerned. How on earth was I to tell her about my period?

It was two days before I eventually plucked up the courage to blurt it out. She seemed scared by the news. She was also shocked, confessing that her own periods hadn't started until she was eighteen. Why was everything happening to me so soon? I had no answer, but at least by the next day I had my own sanitary protection – and my own 'teen bra'.

Within a year or so, a lot of the girls at my school had acquired boyfriends and those of them who hadn't gained respect before had it now. Interest in my clowning around had waned, and with it my popularity. I was out of fashion in more ways than one, with my hedge of dark, frizzy hair that required not so much trimming as topiary. It wasn't a good look when everybody aspired to long, straight hair that swung in long, glossy curtains, like Twiggy's. I spent hours every day trying to iron my hair until I found some heated tongs that did the trick. But they burned my neck and other schoolgirls accused me of having love bites. Wishing that were true, I never put them right.

Half woman, half child, I was full of contradictions. I didn't seem to fit in anywhere any more. Going to grammar school had driven a wedge between me and my primary school friends and now it was driving a wedge between me and my parents as well. I was beginning to feel too East End for school and too West End for home. I'd always enjoyed a good debate with my father, who had a great respect for Parliament and was a staunch believer in people standing up for what was right. But as I got into my history studies, I found I was overtaking him in terms of the ammunition I was able to bring to some of these arguments. He admired Henry VIII for rebelling against the Pope, for example, and I picked holes in his reasoning by pointing out that Henry only rebelled against the Catholic faith when he wanted a new wife to produce an heir. He was chuffed that I was learning, but often what I was being taught conflicted with his own views.

My insecurity manifested itself in rebellion, principally against CFS and its suffocating restrictions. My partner in crime was June, a classmate who lived in a council house near me and who was trying to cope with a troubled home life. Her mother had recently left home and she felt abandoned. Riding the bus together to and from school, we recognised each other as kindred spirits. We shared a lack of respect for authority and an ability to lose ourselves in stories and our own imaginations. We swapped favourite books. I gave her *The Grapes of Wrath*, John Steinbeck's gripping account of the exodus of dirt-poor farmers from the dust bowl of Oklahoma to the 'promised land' of California, and June introduced me to the realm of fantastic creatures in Tolkien's *The Lord of the Rings*, in which she sought solace.

By the fifth form, June and I had come to view CFS less as a seat of learning and more as a stage for St Trinian's-style pranks. Stink bombs were manufactured with sulphuric acid pinched from the chemistry room, chairs placed on ballcocks to create floods. We stole wet clay from the pottery class and pelted student teachers with it when their backs were turned. We justified this bad behaviour by claiming to be anarchists – and in a sense we were. There was a seam of chaos running through each of our lives. I went to bed every night on our living-room sofa and felt the lack of privacy far more keenly as a teenager than I had when I was small. Without a room of my own, I found it virtually impossible to bring friends home. I was ashamed, too, of the slum conditions in which we lived and frustrated that there was no sign of any change in our circumstances. June's mum had left her in the care of a father with whom she constantly fought and with a young brother she was often expected to look after.

In some ways, my father's questioning, probing nature probably instilled in me the idea that rebellion was essentially a good thing. So it was somewhat ironic that I was rebelling in the one place where he wanted me to toe the line. The trouble was, I wasn't always sure exactly what I was challenging. Like Brando's character in *The Wild One*, if someone had asked me what I was rebelling against, I would probably have replied, 'What have you got?'

Perhaps the global atmosphere of unrest in 1968 – the year of revolution – was another influence. In March an anti-Vietnam War protest outside the US Embassy in Grosvenor Square, in the heart of Mayfair, degenerated into a fierce confrontation between demonstrators and police, resulting in 200 arrests. Then, in May, a student protest in Paris escalated into riots on a much bigger scale and led to a general strike involving half the French workforce that crippled the country. Soon students and workers everywhere, from Prague to Chicago to Mexico City, were taking to the streets. June and I felt frustrated that we weren't old enough to join them.

But we were on our own collision course with authority. One afternoon, as we made our way back to school after our lunch break, a couple of barrowboys from the market started throwing fruit at us. We fought back and a pitched battle ensued. The headmistress, hearing the commotion in the street, pulled us into her office and accused us of disgracing the school. Having delivered her dressing-down she allowed June to go but kept me back for another tirade. In an angry speech that seemed to sum up my whole school career, she berated me for wasting every opportunity I'd been offered. If I'd been bright enough to pass the Eleven-Plus, she said, I was bright enough to gain five O-Levels. After that, two A-Levels would see me into university. Moreover, the fact that I had won the Alleyn Award was a clear indication that if I worked hard I might get into Oxbridge. Didn't I want my name on the board outside her office along with those of the cream of our old girls?

Watching her as she continued in this vein, I became suddenly and acutely aware that there was more to this diatribe than a teacher lecturing a pupil. It was someone on the other side of the class divide reminding me of my place and of how lucky I was to be at her precious school. She expected respect but understood nothing about my home life and my situation.

Insolent to the last, I said nothing.

My silence was the final insult. 'Go on. Get out of here and waste your life,' she said. I turned for the door and as I grasped the handle, she added viciously: 'You'll probably be pregnant by the time you're sixteen.'

I turned and looked at her, outraged. Perhaps she thought I'd been flirting with the market boys but I decided against putting her right. If university meant more of this, more blind kowtowing to outdated traditions and heavy-handed authority, I wanted nothing to do with it.

Soon a new interest began to eclipse my studies: pop music. I'd been a Beatles fan since the age of eleven, having screamed through their first two films – *A Hard Day's Night* and, the following year, *Help!* – in the stalls of the Mile End Odeon. Now, as a teenager, I was going to real concerts with live acts. I was besotted by the Walker Bothers and Donovan. I was there when Jimi Hendrix accidentally set fire to his Afro while plucking his guitar strings with his teeth on stage at the Finsbury Park Astoria. I was suffering very badly from crushes on pop stars, probably because I had no access to real boys. Having spent five years at an all-girls' school, I didn't yet know a single boy of my own age. That omission, however, was about to be rectified.

In the summer of 1968 I was asked to be bridesmaid at a neighbour's wedding. For weeks I was caught up in the preparations for the big day, going off to fittings for a white satin dress with pink bolero top. I learned how to stand with a bouquet in my hand and bought a demi-hairpiece – half a head of long, straight hair stuck on a black velvet band. No one suspected it wasn't my own, or so I believed. All of a sudden I found myself mixing with young adults and involved in social activities that felt much more grown-up than mucking about with my schoolmates. The bride and groom were in their late teens and after their marriage would be renting the flat above the groom's mother's. Having friends a few years older than myself with their own flat seemed incredibly sophisticated.

At the wedding rehearsal I met the best man, a young friend of the groom. Martin was just eighteen, tall and lean with long legs like Clint Eastwood's. He seemed just as shy around me as I was in his company, and we didn't say much to each other then, but we continued to meet regularly at the newlyweds' flat. We flirted, exchanging furtive glances across the room.

I was nearly sixteen and for some time Aunt Carrie had been asking me, 'When are you going to find yourself a nice boyfriend?' It was a question my parents had never once put to me. As far as they were concerned, boys were still off limits. 'There'll be plenty of time for all that when you've finished studying,' my father would say. So I had no intention of admitting to them that I had my eye on somebody.

I hadn't even gone on a date with Martin when he walked me home one night from our friends' place and kissed me at the doorstep. Straight away I knew it was love.

After that first kiss Martin and I started 'going out' together. Actually, we didn't go out so much as stay in. Mostly we'd sit in his living room or bedroom playing records. The music of the time said it all. 'It's your thing – do what you wanna do. I can't tell you who to sock it to,' as the Isley Brothers put it.

In the background Northern Ireland's social and political issues, a constant source of debate in our Protestant-Catholic home, were simmering like a pressure cooker waiting to explode. In the spring of 1969 I was pleased to see twenty-one-year-old Bernadette Devlin – dubbed 'Fidel Castro in a mini-skirt' by some

Protestants – become Britain's youngest-ever woman MP when she was elected by Mid-Ulster on a 'Unity' ticket. But that summer the Battle of the Bogside would mark the start of the 'Troubles' and bring the British army to the streets of Northern Ireland. For my mother the matter was clear cut: she sided instinctively with the Catholic cause. My father, however, had a foot in both camps. The IRA were the rebels, and therefore deserving of his support, but in this instance it was his government they were rebelling against, which left him in a bit of a quandary. When it came to the personal versus the political, I was learning, things were not always as straightforward as they seemed.

His primary concern in those years, however, was still the fate of the Royal Mint. Matters had been brought to a head by the government's decision to introduce decimal currency in 1971. The changeover would require millions of new coins to be struck, and in 1967 their proposal to build a new facility at Llantrisant in South Wales was made public. The idea was to gradually phase out production at Tower Hill and transfer the entire Royal Mint to Wales – a plan that my father strongly opposed on behalf of the colleagues he represented.

As the 1960s drew to a close my friends and I moved on from mini-skirts and tight boots to kaftans and sandals. I bought Indian bells to wear about my neck from a shop called Indiacraft in Tottenham Court Road and finally gave up on the straightening tongs: curls and frizz were fashionable now, and it was a relief to be able to leave my hair to do its own thing. I would wander around the Biba store in Kensington High Street, at that time an art-nouveau doll's house filled with clothes, make-up and perfume. I badly wanted to be different and original but so did everyone else, which meant we all wandered around Biba and ended up looking very much the same.

When Martin managed to get tickets for us to see Arthur Brown, whose single 'Fire' had become an alternative hit, I wore black, accessorised by my demi-hairpiece and plenty of startling dark eye shadow – the appropriate style of dress, I felt, for witnessing Arthur erupting on to the stage in his signature flaming metal helmet. Everyone knew about the incident that had taken place the year before at the Windsor Jazz Festival when methanol fuel, accidentally poured over Arthur's head, had caught fire. Luckily, two members of the audience had doused the flames with whatever was to hand, which happened to be beer. Now we all waited with bated breath to see if the experience would be repeated. We were disappointed.

Martin lived about a half a mile away from Lefevre Road. His parents were divorced and his Irish mother, Bridie, worked night shifts as a hospital receptionist. His flat was larger than ours so once she had left for the evening we had the space – and the freedom – to do things I couldn't do at home, but it was all relatively innocent. Martin's room was something to behold. The walls were lined with posters of Jimi Hendrix, T-Rex and Led Zeppelin, all bathed in the glow of a red light bulb. A stolen British Rail safety lamp sat in pride of place in a corner and on the ceiling were cutting-edge polystyrene tiles. We spent a long time looking up at them, smoking either designer cigarettes like Sobranie or Du Maurier or very weak joints that quite possibly contained henna rather than cannabis. We wouldn't have known the difference.

With his lean build and delicate features, Martin was in every way the antithesis of my father. He wore his curly hair like Bob Dylan's on the cover of the *Blonde on Blonde* album, and was generous with his meagre wages as an apprentice with the Gas Board, buying me jewellery and bottles of Aqua Manda perfume which made me smell like an orange. He had left school after taking his O-Levels and found gas-fitting incredibly boring. His parents' divorce was hard for him to accept and when we visited his father one afternoon, I could tell, just by the way Martin looked at him, how much he missed having his dad in his life.

I began to see Martin most evenings and in time his flat came to feel more like home than mine. My parents didn't approve of me going out so often, especially when I began staying out increasingly late. They wanted me to concentrate on my schoolwork. To my dad, education was everything. 'You could work in a bank!' he said enthusiastically, in an effort to inspire me. It was his idea of a respectable, steady job with prospects and a good

pension but exactly how he envisaged it bringing fulfil-
ment to him or to me I can't imagine. His expectations
of me were fierce but unfocused. My parents simply
wanted a better life for me than the one they had, but
while I was struggling to discover what I wanted for
myself I felt constantly under pressure.

I never actually told them where I was going or who
I was seeing but, not surprisingly, they guessed there
was a boy involved. When a neighbour told my mother
she had seen a handsome young man walking me home
one night, she didn't sit me down to discuss sex or
contraception. Instead she simply insisted point-blank
that the relationship should end. To me this seemed
unreasonable, so I ignored her edict, but from then on
when I went to Martin's I pretended to be visiting June.

My best friend now seemed to come and go as she
pleased with little parental supervision. She and her
father had reached an accommodation: they just avoided
each other. June appeared to be reacting to her mother's
absence by developing an eating disorder. Looking
back, she displayed all the symptoms of anorexia,
though at the time it wasn't a word we'd ever heard.

After six months, my mother backed off. Perhaps she
was in denial about my relationship with Martin;
perhaps she had decided to trust me to be sensible. My
father, however, remained outraged about the late
nights I kept.

One evening when I was round at Martin's there was
a knock on the front door. Bridie was in, too, as it was

her night off, and she opened it to find my mother on her doorstep, upset and pleading for me to come home. It transpired that she had argued with my father, who was blaming her for having no 'proper control'. Bridie calmed her down, reassuring her that there was no cause for concern. She convinced my mother there was nothing to fear from her son. Martin was a good boy, she said. He and I were dating, it was all perfectly normal at our age and he would always walk me back to our flat.

As I watched my mother walking off into the night, I felt sorry for her but at the same time I was angry and embarrassed that she had turned up on my boyfriend's doorstep. I was keeping two lives separate and I wanted them to stay that way. I couldn't see that any good would come from introducing Martin to my parents. I did not wish to hear their opinion of him because I knew they wouldn't approve of him on principle. I would be taking my O-Levels in a few months' time and it was expected that I would stay on, study for my A-Levels and then apply to a university. Any boy, whether it was Martin or somebody else, would only be regarded as a threat to that.

But I had already made my decision. I wasn't going to finish with Martin and I wasn't going to pander to my headmistress. My name would never appear on the board outside her office because I was going to walk out straight after my exams and take a job. Any job.

My parents were disappointed when they failed to persuade me to change my mind, but there wasn't much they could do about it. I passed six O-Levels and left school almost to spite the headmistress and the system. I didn't even bother to go in on the last day of term to say goodbye to my teachers. I felt fully justified in leaving them and their rigid, outmoded education behind me. I already knew more than they did. Or so I thought.

Chapter Five

Keeping Secrets

June left school at the same time as I did – we had always planned to 'bust out' together. But, having made our grand gesture, our resolve dissipated and we mooched around for a month or so, claiming we were looking for a job. In truth we weren't doing much to find one.

Towards the end of the summer June's father went off on holiday, taking her younger brother with him. She asked me if I would stay with her some nights to keep her company. My mother couldn't see anything untoward in this: June was one of only two friends I had ever invited into our home, so she was a known quantity. She lived only five minutes away and I came back regularly, sometimes bringing her with me. To my parents it all seemed innocent but they didn't know that June and I were helping ourselves to her father's best Navy rum and playing music as loud as we could,

Terry Reid's gravelly blues voice booming 'Stay with Me, Baby' morning, noon and night.

Martin would come round to June's when he finished work. One night he stayed over and we slept together for the first time. We had been an item for over six months, there were no parents around and it just felt right, as if we were a grown-up couple sharing a 'pad' of our own. We should have used protection but we didn't. We weren't ignorant about contraception. I'd learned about sex at primary school: when we were nine my friend 'Sticky' Sickelmore had explained how babies came from 'ladies' virginias'. Some years later, further sex education at CFS had filled in any biological blanks. I was aware that I was at a stage of my menstrual cycle that wasn't conducive to conception. Surely it wasn't called the safe period for nothing? Being young and in love made us feel somehow inviolate, too. What could go wrong?

I waved Martin off to work the next morning and went back to Lefevre Road. Was it possible, I wondered, that my parents could tell what I had done? I studied myself in the mirror. My face looked unchanged and yet everything was different. I was no longer a virgin.

That evening I sat watching television with them. Nothing seemed amiss and nothing was said. No one knew. I was very relieved. But when my next period was due, there was no sign of it. I confided in June and she told me that hers had stopped completely. I would

later realise that this was probably because of her eating disorder, but neither of us understood that at the time. Mine had always been irregular so I told myself there were all sorts of reasons why I might be late.

Any anxiety I may have had was completely eclipsed by some other news: finally, nineteen years after my parents first put their names on the council list, we were going to be rehoused. None of us could quite believe this until we were given a selection of flats to choose from. My father said he didn't mind where we went as long as my mother and I were happy. We viewed one show home after another before opting for 23 Gullane House, an upper maisonette on a nearby estate. It boasted a kitchen at the front and a spacious sitting room with windows all along one wall. Upstairs was a double bedroom, store cupboard, separate toilet, bathroom and, most importantly, a second bedroom, complete with a built-in wardrobe. We gratefully took charge of the keys.

The night before we moved in, I secretly took Martin to see my new home. Having recently ditched his Gas Board apprenticeship owing to terminal boredom and started work on a building site, he now considered himself a bit of an expert on house design and he wasn't overly impressed. He didn't much care for the convection heating system with its ugly vent into the sitting room or the rough plaster finish on the walls. I made noises of agreement but really I couldn't have cared less. All that mattered to me was that, for the first time in my life, I had a room I could call my own.

My parents and I cleared our belongings from the house at Lefevre Road, leaving behind only memories. In transit I lost my treasured Olivetti typewriter but I had plenty to keep me occupied. I painted the walls of my room olive green and yellow and luxuriated in my first double bed, which I covered with a bri-nylon quilt to match the decor. Seeing so much enthusiasm for interior design, my parents rashly allowed me to decorate and furnish the whole flat. From a store in Roman Road I chose a black plastic three-piece suite, a Formica sideboard with co-ordinating table and chairs, a low coffee table with a well in the middle for magazines and a large red vase, in which I arranged sheaves of wheat. My *pièce de résistance* was a huge reproduction painting of a white horse beneath a waterfall. I insisted the white-painted walls remained as they were to show this off to its best advantage.

My parents viewed my efforts open-mouthed. They were lovers of patterned carpet and textured wallpaper so it was all a bit of a shock. To my chagrin, kitsch items began to sneak in, notably a small statue of a Native American chief wearing a litmus-paper outfit that forecast the weather and bore the legend: 'Apron blue – sky is too. Apron pink – weather stink!'

As soon as we moved in, my mother stopped going to the Bridge House and I realised just how much of a safety valve the pub had been for her. She had lived on her nerves at Lefevre Road but now, with room to breathe and a sense of security, I knew she felt we could be a proper family in a proper home. Everything was perfect – or would have been perfect if only my period would come.

Meanwhile, June and I had found jobs together in 'press publicity' at a Farringdon agency, which to us sounded impossibly glamorous. What the work actually entailed was somewhat more mundane. We would be given lists of names – celebrities, politicians, sports personalities, and the great and the good – and sat all day in a large office sifting through piles of newspapers, identifying any articles about or references to our subjects, cutting them out and sticking them on to pieces of paper. For ten minutes or so in every hour, a radio would switch on automatically to signal the arrival of 'Smoky Joe Time', when we were allowed to break off for a cigarette. Presumably it wasn't safe to permit smoking all the time with so much paper about. We'd thought we were on the way to seeking our fortunes, but what we were doing barely even qualified as an office job – it was really only one step up from working in a factory. Still, experiencing an early reality check on our high-flown ambitions was probably good for us.

I soon had far bigger concerns than my job. By the spring of 1970, I knew for certain I was pregnant. Yet while my condition remained unconfirmed I somehow managed to carry on pretending nothing was wrong.

Even the morning sickness I'd suffered in the winter hadn't prompted me to act. In time it had passed and as soon as I felt better, I convinced myself everything was fine.

I may have prided myself on being a mature adult but in truth I was barely out of my childhood – it was only a matter of months since I'd been chucking stink bombs around a classroom – and I responded to the situation like a child. I simply ignored it and hoped it would go away, even though on an intellectual level I knew that was never going to happen. Unlike the swollen women I saw lumbering through the market, I didn't even look pregnant, which made it all the easier to exist in state of denial. The only perceptible change in my body was the appearance of a little pot belly.

I had given up my job at the cuttings agency when the morning sickness had taken hold, causing me to turn up late or call in sick too often. For the next four or five months of my pregnancy I remained unemployed, though I can't remember how I got my parents to acquiesce to that without too many complaints. I must have told them I'd been laid off and was having trouble finding another job. They didn't seem too concerned as they could see I was keeping myself busy. I was still doing my Laurence Llewellyn-Bowen number on our maisonette and handling the housework as well, so my mum was only too pleased to be coming back to a tidy home in the evenings for the first time in her married life.

Nobody knew my secret except for Martin and June. How could I possibly break something like this to my mother when it had taken me two days to tell her I'd started my periods? Now that I had a room to myself I had more privacy, so I was managing to hide any weight gain beneath kaftans and other baggy clothes. My parents evidently didn't suspect a thing. But one day I felt a sudden lurch inside me. The baby was moving.

By sheer coincidence, I knew two other girls who were also pregnant. Carol and Hazel were the girl-friends of a couple of Martin's mates and part of our social circle. But their reaction couldn't have been more different from mine. They were over the moon. I listened, mute, as they chattered excitedly about their pregnancies, debated the merits of various names and compared notes. Hazel was about to get married; Carol was already engaged and the only modification she and her fiancé needed to make to their plans for the future was to bring their wedding forward by a few months for form's sake. They reminded me of my friends at primary school and their mothers, who accepted that having children was what everybody did: when babies came along, you greeted them with joy, loved them and just took them in your stride. But Hazel was two or three years older than me and both girls had homes and partners with steady jobs. Martin, on the other hand, was working as a casual labourer and I was just seven-teen and unemployed. We had nothing except each other. We had every desire to stay together but any possibility of marriage and setting up on our own was some way in the future.

Being with Hazel and Carol at that time was like having a mirror constantly held up to me but still I refused to look into it and face facts. After five missed periods I was too far gone for a termination and Martin and I now saw only one solution: adoption. To us the pregnancy seemed not so much about a living, breathing baby as a mistake we had made, a mistake that had to be put right before we could continue with our lives. Just as I had done as a small child, I was problem-solving in a clinical, superficially adult way and not allowing my feelings to intervene. I still wasn't emotionally mature enough to do otherwise.

Perhaps if I'd talked to my parents, if we'd sat down and discussed everything, it might have been different. But the question I was asking wasn't 'Can we possibly do this?', it was 'How can I possibly tell my parents?', and I couldn't get beyond that. I couldn't bear to imagine the look of disappointment on my father's face or the sight of my mother's tears. There would be no more bragging from my dad about his kid, that was for sure. So much for expectations.

My only option, I reasoned, was to present them with a fait accompli: 'I'm pregnant – but it's OK, don't worry. Everything's sorted, the baby will be adopted and we can go back to normal. Nobody need ever know.' I even allowed myself to consider that I might be able to get through the whole thing without them ever finding out.

Eventually Hazel was told of our plans. She couldn't understand how Martin and I could ever consider adoption. She persuaded me to make an appointment to see the doctor.

Dr Teverson was still my family's GP, as he had been for almost all my life, making visits to our flat throughout my childhood, braving a terrible winter one year to find me seriously ill on the sofa with bronchitis. That evening his glasses had misted up in the heat from our old paraffin heater and as he peered over the top of their cloudy lenses, he had gravely warned my parents to invest in a mains heater or lose me to pleurisy. My mother and father had always been grateful for his advice and deferential to his position, especially since their previous doctor, a woman, had been notoriously harsh and unsympathetic. When my mother was nine months' pregnant, she had gone to her practice with grotesquely swollen ankles, asking if she could possibly have a certificate for the last week of her pregnancy since her job was swinging hundredweight bags of coins on to trucks at the Royal Mint. This martinet had lectured her about pregnancy not being an illness, forcing her to work right up to the birth.

Now, eight years after our kind family doctor had diagnosed my puberty, I was sitting in the same surgery having a teenage pregnancy confirmed. It was no surprise, but it came as a shock none the less to have it spelled out to me that I was already six months' pregnant. Dr Teverson told me that I would have to begin attending the hospital immediately and, after taking my blood pressure, he sat down to write up his notes. My eyes were drawn to the shelf above his desk. On it sat a tall jar, filled with a variety of boiled sweets – acid drops, humbugs, cough candies. Over the years he had taken down the jar to offer me a sweet every time I had cried or seemed anxious. I heard myself suddenly blurting out that the baby I was expecting would have to be adopted.

Dr Teverson stopped writing and looked at me across his glasses. I met his gaze.

'I can't keep the baby. It's impossible.'

For a moment he was silent. I looked away, tortured by a mixture of embarrassment and guilt.

Having briefly reflected on what I'd said, he explained that I would need to discuss that further with a medical social worker at the maternity hospital. He returned to his writing and when he had finished he handed me a referral letter. The sweet jar remained on the shelf.

Dazed, I walked out of the surgery and on to the street. It was real at last. I was going to have a baby. The denial stage was over and I was entering the next phase of my pregnancy: blind panic.

That night, at home, I watched my parents involved in their usual routines: my father eating supper on his lap, railing against the television news; my mother quietly occupied in the kitchen, catching up with her housework. My heart was thumping but inside my body another, tiny heart was softly beating. I could ignore it no longer. After an hour or so, I headed upstairs to my room, telling my parents I needed an early night.

A few days later, I received notification of a hospital appointment. I had been booked in at the Mothers' Hospital in Clapton Road, Hackney, which, I would discover, was run by the Salvation Army – a successor to a series of maternity homes they had set up at the end of the nineteenth century for unmarried mothers as an alternative to the workhouse. Services at the Mothers' Hospital, opened in 1913, had always been available to all mothers, although in accordance with the Salvation Army's aims it had a particular remit to care for those who were single or poor. And having kept its Salvation Army identity after being integrated into the National Health Service, it also retained that bias.

Hazel insisted on coming along with me to my first appointment. She was determined to change my mind about the adoption and, like a newlywed threatened by a singleton, she refused to entertain any of my misgivings about teenage motherhood. She was unwavering in her confidence that where there's a will, there's a way.

The medical social worker, middle-aged and reserved, seemed sympathetic. At any rate she treated me with compassion as I told her my story. I explained that I was still living at home but had succeeded, thus far, in keeping the pregnancy from my parents. Hazel offered up the view that I wouldn't be able to do so for much longer. I countered by voicing the possibility I'd been nurturing that I might be able to give birth and have my baby adopted without anyone ever knowing at all. As soon as the words were out of my mouth I realised how ridiculous this idea sounded but the social worker listened without comment. I wasn't worried that she would give away my secret. I knew I was protected by the rules of patient confidentiality and so did she. She told me she would set things in motion for the adoption.

At the time I wasn't aware that a lot of the staff at the hospital were Salvation Army officers, but as we said goodbye to the social worker, I could have sworn I saw a bonnet hanging on the back of her door.

Outside on the pavement, Hazel stared at me, appalled. 'It won't be as easy as you think,' she warned. 'You have to consider the baby. Even if you're with him for just a short while in hospital, he'll fret for you. He'll miss your smell.' This was the last thing I wanted to hear. I went to the rest of my hospital appointments alone.

A few weeks later, Martin and I learned that the medical social worker had set up a meeting for us with a justice of the peace to discuss the adoption. We took the tube to North London and made our way to a sprawling house in a leafy part of Hampstead.

A woman opened the door with a genial smile. She was in her early fifties, short and dark-haired, and radiated a bustling self-confidence. Showing us into a book-lined room looking out over a beautiful garden, she sat us down, gave us tea and began to ask us questions, inquiring into our backgrounds, religions and academic histories, making notes as we responded. Finally, she put down her pen and told us that she was in close contact with a couple who, she believed, would make perfect parents for our baby.

Sitting beside Martin as the JP talked, I felt incredibly young and insignificant. Taking in the elegant desk stacked with papers, I was transported back to my headmistress's office. During the dressing-down she had given me I'd been angry and indignant, considering myself far too old to be insulted in this patronising manner. Now, conscious that I was in the wrong, I felt guilty, penitent and intimidated by my 'betters'. I had done exactly what she had predicted I would do, and it was a bitter pill to swallow.

The JP was warning us that once the adoption was legally completed there could be no further contact with our baby. In some cases, adoptive parents might see fit to send on news to a child's birth parents but only through an intermediary. In this case, since the prospective adoptive mother had been in the public eye, and her own father well known in his professional field, it was deemed to be both unfair and unwise for us ever to know who they might be. Did we understand?

I nodded, but I wasn't fully able to absorb the ramifications of what she was trying to tell us: that we would never see our child again, as infant or adult, since at that time adopted children did not have a legal right to access their original birth certificates or other records. She went on to explain that this couple lived in a large house with a lovely garden. I looked again out of the latticed window. Perhaps they had a house like this. It was becoming clear they were successful and financially secure, far better equipped to give my unborn baby a good life than Martin and I were at present, and probably ever would be.

I knew all my parents wanted for me was a better life than theirs. It didn't occur to me until much later that I was transferring the same undefined ambitions to my baby. He would be better off with this couple purely because they were my 'betters'. I was as convinced of that as I was that our baby was a boy.

The JP was smiling kindly. Although there could be no more contact, she said, she would try to persuade the adoptive parents to send me a single photograph, just to show that our baby was doing well. Until then I should take care of myself until the child was born.

I went to the hospital each month for check-ups. As my due date approached, I gained the impression the doctors thought something wasn't quite right. I was still very small – my bump hardly showed at all – and they were beginning to wonder whether I had got my dates wrong. I was adamant that they were correct. In

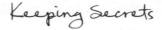

the end, it was decided that I should attend the hospital every week for treatment in an experimental machine designed to help increase the blood supply to the womb.

During these sessions I sat encased in a piece of futuristic equipment that put pressure on my abdomen using some kind of suction. I resented having to undergo this treatment, not just because it was uncomfortable, but because it seemed to be working: one afternoon my father remarked that I was putting on weight. But if he harboured any suspicions that I might be pregnant, he was in denial, too. Neither he nor my mother ever tackled me on the subject.

I was still visiting Martin most evenings, and he was still walking me home as usual, kissing me goodnight by the rubbish chute on the landing. But we had started to argue. I was stressed, my moods were erratic and I had crying jags. I began to question the unquestionable: could we possibly keep the baby? Could we move in with Bridie, or my parents? Unable to think clearly any longer, one night I decided that Martin and I should break up.

We didn't see each other for a week or so. Then he wrote me a long letter clearly setting out his feelings and reviewing the plans we had made. He wrote that he still loved me but that he was convinced having our baby adopted was the right decision. We'd always acknowledged that the conception had been a mistake, and nothing had happened since then to change anything. Now we just had to do what we could to make it right, and keeping the baby just because he was 'our baby' was selfish. We had to consider what was best for him. We were too young, we had no money and we had nowhere to live. We both knew that a baby deserved much more than what we had to offer and here was a rich couple waiting in the wings to give him everything he would ever need.

His measured words put everything into perspective. I realised I had been toying with alternatives rather than seriously considering them.

How did I think I was going to bring up a baby in my room? My parents had looked forward for years to having a home of their own, never dreaming they might need it to accommodate an unmarried daughter and her baby. I tried to imagine the scene, all of us trapped together in one council flat. I would be reliant on my mum and dad, emotionally and financially, perhaps forever.

Somewhere beyond the East End there was something called the 'permissive society', but it hadn't filtered through to Gullane House. Here, on this estate, people still adhered to a strict social code. They might not have had money but they still had morals and clean doorsteps. Shotgun marriages were not yet a thing of the past. I thought of my mother, beaten for talking to boys on street corners. She had known she must never bring shame on her family and neither could I.

And what would happen to Martin and me if I insisted on keeping the baby? I didn't want to lose him,

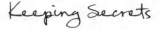

but that was quite likely to be the outcome. I knew in my heart that everything he had said in his letter was true. And so, adrift in a sea of hormones and powerful emotions, I clung on to Martin, held fast to the conviction that we were doing the right thing and wiped all other ideas from my mind.

A few days after this crisis I have a visitor. It is June, thinner and more frail than ever, dressed in crushed velvet and wearing a headband tied across her forehead. In her carpet bag she carries a collection of books, not Tolkien now but Camus, Kerouac and Sartre. She tells me that she is off on the hippy trail. She is going to hitch-hike her way to Marrakesh to sample life on the road. She feels bad about not being with me for the birth, but…

I understand completely. June has to follow her own path and I am glad she has found the courage to break away from the East End and her difficult home life to go in search of the world of opportunities we've read about and talked about constantly since we first became friends. When it's time for her to go, we stand up and she smiles a little sadly. I step forward and hug her, holding her close. Her long, auburn hair smells of patchouli oil and cannabis. I wish her the best of luck and tell her to keep herself safe.

At the end of May, as I attended my final pre-natal appointments at the Mothers' Hospital, 'In the Summertime' by the previously little-known band Mungo Jerry seemed to be playing everywhere I went.

Within a fortnight of its release it would top the charts, going on to become the bestselling single of the year. Something about this bluesy shuffle, with its hypnotic riff and jaunty lyrics, encapsulated the carefree days of summer, and everyone was singing along to it. I wanted so much to join in but I was in the grip of a rising sense of panic. I had so little time to go now. I just needed to keep my secret for a few more weeks, but if I grew any bigger, my parents were going to find out whether I wanted them to or not.

Chapter Six

Ten Short Days

A black plastic zip-up suitcase, normally used for family holidays, was already packed and safely hidden under my bed. It contained all I thought I would need for my stay in hospital – nightwear, sanitary towels, wash bag, towel and face cloth, Astral soap and as many baby clothes as I'd been able to afford to buy with my weekly pocket money and donations from Martin. Everything had been planned with military precision. As soon as I went into labour I would take myself off to the Mothers' Hospital, sneaking out in the middle of the night if need be. Martin would come round to see my parents, collect the suitcase and break the news to them. We had every angle covered. Or so we thought.

What we hadn't foreseen was that my mother would not go to work that day. But when the time came, for some reason she felt unwell and stayed at home. My mother was seldom unwell, and never took a day off, even when she had a terrible cold. This was the woman, remember, who was heaving massive sacks of coins around at the Royal Mint only hours before giving birth to me and, physically at least, she was made of strong stuff. Perhaps some sixth sense had told her she should remain at home – my father had always said she was psychic, after all.

By lunchtime, I was aware that something was happening. I felt a sudden gush of blood, unfamiliar to me since my periods had stopped. I went upstairs to investigate. I had no pain and the bleeding had ceased but I knew this was a 'show'. I had to get to the hospital.

I walked down the stairs as casually as I could and picked up my jacket from its hook near the front door. My mother's voice followed me from the kitchen.

'Where are you going?'

I paused. What should I say?

'To the hospital.'

My mother appeared, wiping her wet hands on a tea towel. 'To see your friend?'

She knew that Hazel had recently had her baby, a little boy. For a moment I considered just nodding my head and walking out of the door, telling her I'd be back later. But my hand was frozen to the door handle. Everything was frozen. My mother and I would be suspended in this tableau until I decided what to do.

'No,' I said eventually. 'I'm going to have a baby myself.'

The words were out – like the baby soon would be – but it was clear that my mum could have had no premonition because her face crumpled before my eyes, as though she'd been slapped. And in a way she had been.

I heard myself reeling off the matter-of-fact speech I had rehearsed in my head so many times. Everything was going to be all right, I told her. I was fully prepared. Martin would drop round later for my suitcase, the baby would be adopted and no one would ever have to know. I was still talking but I was out of the door now and my legs were carrying me along the balcony. Glancing back, I saw that my mother was crying. 'No one needs to know!' I called out to her.

I turned away and hurried down the stairs, past the rubbish chute and out on to the street. It was only then that I realised Martin would be at work and I wouldn't be able to reach him immediately. This wouldn't have mattered if I'd managed to get to the hospital without my mother finding out, but now I needed to warn him that she had.

The chaos of that day illustrates just how out of our depth Martin and I really were. Our childlike scheme had more holes in it than a leaky watering can. How could it have been otherwise when my overriding concern was that I shouldn't have to be the one to tell my parents? That was the worst thing I could possibly imagine. Now the unimaginable had happened and my mother knew. But Martin didn't. Everything was the wrong way round. Nothing was working out as we had planned. I was in a panic and worried about Martin. The only way of getting a message to him was through Bridie. Telling her wouldn't be so bad – I'd cleared the worst hurdle, and she was less uptight than my mother – but even so this wasn't the kind of news I could break to her from a public callbox. So I walked the half-mile to her flat.

Bridie should have been sleeping in readiness for her night shift but when I rang the bell she opened the door straight away. We went upstairs to the living room and had sat down on the sofa before I told her I was having a baby. Martin's baby. Right now. She gaped at me, stunned. How could we have kept this secret for so long? I gave her the same speech I'd given my mother. She wasn't angry but there was sadness, so much sadness that she wept a little. 'My first grand-child,' she said tearfully, 'and I shan't even see him grow up.'

Any apprehension I might have had about the birth itself was draining away now, to be replaced by a crushing guilt about the pain I was causing. The two worlds I'd been struggling to keep separate – truth and pretence – had collided catastrophically and amid the fallout everything seemed so more starkly real than it had before. I left Bridie crying and took a bus to Clapton Pond. I had no idea what the labour was going to be

like but one thing of which I could be certain was that there would be drama to follow.

At the hospital I was examined by a busy doctor who decided I was overdue. She explained that the membrane surrounding my 'waters' had hardened and would need to be perforated with an instrument called an amnihook to fully induce labour.

My legs are strapped in stirrups and I feel so vulnerable – especially when I see something resembling a crochet hook in the doctor's hand. The agony is far worse than anything I will feel during labour. After the procedure, I am put in a room on my own but I can still hear women's voices screaming all around me. The pain from the induction subsides and metamorphoses into a new ordeal. Although I am in full labour now, I am strangely relieved to be alone. I tell myself that everything I am experiencing is natural. I am not ill, I am just going through a process. It will be all right. I will survive.

A few hours pass. I can see the light beginning to fade outside the window. The room is suddenly busy. I am given gas and air and more people come, telling me what to do. I obey. I push and push. Now they are warning me, saying they need to cut me. The episiotomy is performed and, eight hours after I have entered this room, a baby is born. Not a boy, I am told, but a beautiful little girl.

I feel the tidal wave of afterbirth, a flush of warmth. Relief. But someone calls for an incubator and there is alarm in her voice. I feel tremendous guilt. If the baby isn't well it must be my fault. I have failed to take proper care of myself and of her. How could she be a girl? How could Martin and I have got things so wrong?

Someone says forget the incubator. I wait, breathless. There is only silence. Then something ethereal: the sound of a baby crying, not insistently, but just enough to declare she is alive. She is placed in my arms. I look down at this stranger. She is nothing like I have imagined. Not a big, bouncing infant like the babies in my schoolfriends' homes – but a frail, fragile creature with an expression as old as time itself. She looks at me, passive. No temper, no demands, her mouth making 'O' shapes like a goldfish.

A few moments later, Martin was there, looking comical in a white gown and face mask. He had brought with him the zip-up suitcase from under my bed so I knew that he had confronted my parents, and under-stood now how much courage that had taken. We both stared in bewilderment at our creation. I was dazed, from gas and air, from exhaustion and from the shock of finding that my secret was now out and lying beside me. It occurred to me that I knew absolutely nothing about how to take care of her. Something more painful than labour kicked in: the realisation that when I walked out of the Mothers' Hospital I would do so leaving our baby behind.

I slept for hours after the birth. When I awoke, on the ward now, a nurse brought my baby to me and showed me how to put her to my breast. I didn't know what I felt: the sense of cold, hard reality I'd had at Bridie's house had gone and I couldn't be sure whether any of this was actually happening or whether I was imagining it. I remembered the scene in *The Grapes of Wrath* in which Rose of Sharon, after giving birth to a stillborn child, allows an old man dying of starvation to suckle at her breast...

A panicked voice cut into my thoughts. Another woman on the other side of the ward was shouting that she had been given the wrong baby. Our infants were inspected and swapped over. This time I checked my baby's wrist tag and saw that it read 'Baby Wassmer'.

When I tried again to feed my baby the ward sister ran in and stopped me, whispering that, because of my circumstances, I should not breastfeed. She gave me pills to dry up my milk. I took one, then watched the other mothers holding their babies close. After a while I put a plastic teat to my own baby's lips and she began to suckle, looking up at me all the while.

Martin visited me the next morning and we decided to name our daughter Sarah Louise. He wanted to give her his surname, knowing it would then go on to her birth certificate. He sat beside my bed, looking first at me and then at his little girl. I could see that, however lost he felt, he was still desperately trying to do the right thing.

Left alone with Sarah Louise, I talked to her, planting soft kisses on the top of her head. Her skin was pale but she was perfect, with long fingernails and wise eyes. She had exceptionally long legs, like her father. It felt as if no one and nothing could touch us, but I knew that was an illusion.

When my parents came to visit me there was a wall of embarrassment between us. There was also a baby's cot. My father looked into it first. I saw his face soften. My mother's, however, was still etched with anxiety. We were casting around for something on which to pin our conversation. How was the food in the hospital? Did I have everything I needed? Much of what we communicated to each other that day remained unspoken. When my father left the ward for a cigarette my mother confided that he had told her I must keep my baby if that was what I wanted. But it seemed significant that he wasn't here, voicing his opinion for himself. Was he too shocked to do so? He had gone off to work the previous morning and returned to find that, out of the blue, his daughter had given birth to a baby. How would he talk to me now? What would he think of me? I looked at my mother. Her eyes entreated me to stay strong and stick to my decision.

'I'm not going to change my mind,' I told her.

She seemed able to breathe again. She would, she assured me, be there for me the day I was discharged.

For ten days I sought refuge in the hospital routine. My new world smelled of milk and nappies, and in my head I heard the voices of my childhood friends: 'Hold my sister for me!' Now the child was mine. There was a camaraderie among the mothers which in some ways reminded me of the school camp I'd gone to with Mrs LeWars's class. We were here only temporarily but each of us knew how special this time was and we were making the most, and the best, of this hiatus in our normal lives. No longer a child, I was adjusting to being a recovering mum, learning how to take care of a baby who looked to me to supply what she needed to live and thrive: food and love.

One day I was holding Sarah Louise, gently kissing her head as I talked quietly to her, when I felt a hole in her skull. Convinced I had blown my kisses clean into her brain, I was filled with panic. For a while I said nothing to anybody but eventually, burdened by guilt, I confessed to another mum. She smiled and told me about the fontanelle, the soft dent in the top of the head all babies have until the bones in their skull knit properly. It would close in time. I listened to her in wonder, relief giving way to a recognition that since her birth there had been nothing between my daughter's mind and the thoughts that I had been planting there in whispers. For a few brief, magical days there had been no barrier between us at all.

In a small room off the ward we were instructed in how to hold our babies properly, how to wind them, change their nappies and bathe them. I remembered the girls at my primary school who had gone on to secondary moderns. Those who had ended up in the layette class would be streaks ahead of me now. I paid attention to everything the nurses told us, acutely aware all the while that this information was going to be of limited use to me, whereas the other mothers would be putting the skills they were learning into practice in the months to come.

The nurses treated us all equally. They must have known I would be giving my baby away but they didn't acknowledge it and there was no overt disapproval. Although they were kind to me I was always waiting for their reproof. One hot afternoon I was on the other side of the ward, talking to another mum, making her laugh, as if I were still the class clown, when a nurse came up behind me and told me to go back to my bed. My baby might need me.

I am a bad mother. I am no mother at all. I am a mother in body only. Sweet liquid continues to seep from my breasts in spite of the tablets I am taking but I'm playing a role. My secret may be out but I am still pretending, and if there were no world beyond these walls I could go on pretending forever.

I was living in the moment, not thinking about the future or even what was happening outside the Mothers' Hospital. The real world invaded when my mother next visited. She brought fruit and filled me in on some of the gaps in the day I had left her on the landing of our building for Bridie's house and the hospital. She recounted how she had run, distraught, to a couple who lived on the floor below us. They were my mother's friends as well as our neighbours: she trusted them not to tell a soul. 'They'll keep your secret,' she said.

Looking at her, I knew it was less my secret than hers. She cared too much about what people thought, especially the people on our new estate.

She then told me something my father had said to her on the night I'd given birth to my baby. 'Poor kid. To have to go through that all alone.' His words didn't make me feel sorry for myself, only for my mum. I understood that she would have taken them as a criticism of her parenting. In our own ways we were both bad mothers. She felt she had failed me and I, in turn, was failing the tiny girl in the cot between us, a child who hardly ever cried.

Technically, I was still in control. I had not signed any documents apart from the birth certificate. When the registrar visited the ward, Martin had dutifully attended and, as we had discussed, gave Sarah Louise his surname. Mine was there too. What is written cannot be unwritten and we were recorded as 'mother' and 'father' for all time. Even though our daughter would never know us as her parents, I was comforted that somewhere a document would always exist, a testament to these days before her new life began.

The June weather grew increasingly hot, French windows were thrown open and I stepped out on to the lawn beyond the ward. It was the first time we had been outside the walls of this hospital since giving birth. I could hear the buzz of traffic on Clapton High Street: the real world out there, calling us back to it. This was the last day I would spend with these women. One by one we were leaving. Tomorrow it would be my turn.

The following morning, I opened my black suitcase, already packed for my departure, and took out a plastic bag. Inside was a tiny white dress ruched with frills and lace. I had seen it in the window of a shop on Roman Road market – the prettiest dress I had been able to afford. I was determined that my child should have at least one beautiful thing to wear so that her new parents could tell her, one day, how much she was loved.

Sarah Louise lay on the bed looking up at me as I peeled off her cotton suit and put on the white dress. Spotless, stainless, perfect: she was already beginning to look like someone else's baby. I returned to the bag for a pair of matching bootees and a woollen shawl so light and soft I could barely feel it. Now swaddled in white, Sarah Louise gazed up at me, content, unfocused.

A nurse arrived to tell me everything was ready. Seeing my hesitation, she took control. 'It's all right,' she said gently. 'Just follow me. Everything will be fine.'

She lifted my suitcase while I gathered up Sarah Louise. I followed the nurse into the room outside the ward where I'd learned how to care for my baby. Today there was no one there, and no baths or towels or talcum powder or nappies, just a single cot.

The nurse put down my case and looked at me calmly, holding out her arms. 'You can give her to me now.'

I know that all I have to do is hand my baby to the nurse. She stands there like a drawbridge between me and my child's new parents. Once I have let go of Sarah Louise, the drawbridge will be pulled up forever, allowing us to go our separate ways.

I notice the nurse's eyes dart towards the door. Someone is there. I hesitate, turning my head. It is not my baby's new parents but my mother, waiting for me on my side of the bridge. She gives me a nervous smile and picks up my suitcase. 'Come on,' she whispers, her voice hoarse with emotion.

I look back at the nurse. Her arms are still outstretched. In my own, Sarah Louise is still passive, oblivious of how her life is about to change irrevocably. Her tiny feet are swamped by the white bootees. Why hadn't I bought smaller ones? They are slipping off as I pass her carefully to the nurse. It is done.

Then my mother and I are walking quickly along a corridor, sunlight streaming through open windows on either side. Someone is coming towards me: another mum is also leaving the hospital today but it takes me a second to recognise her in her summer dress.

As we meet she registers the suitcase my mother is carrying. 'Are you off now?' she asks me. Her smile is as bright as the bold colours of her dress. But suddenly a shadow flickers across her face. She knows there is something wrong, something is missing.

'Where is your baby?'

I have no idea what to say. The woman waits, confused by my silence. Both she and my mother are looking at me expectantly and I know I have to give an answer but then, suddenly, a nurse is hurrying past us with a bundle of clothes: a white shawl and a white ruched dress. The woman's eyes are still on me but I am staring after the nurse, watching her round a corner, wondering where she has taken my baby's clothes. I hear myself reply: 'I left her behind.'

The young woman's face instantly clouds. As a mother, she cannot make sense of what I have told her. I feel hot tears streaming down my face, the first I have shed since giving birth. My own mother looks at me helplessly in the same way I looked at her as a child, anguished and impotent in the face of her grief, the pain of being separated from her beloved brother.

'Don't cry,' she says as she takes my hand. We walk on together as the young mum gapes after us, speechless.

Outside, on the hot street, a man stepped smartly out of a parked car and opened the passenger doors for us. It was the husband of the couple who lived on the floor below us, the friends in whom my mother had confided. He knew my secret. But he didn't speak of it. Instead he nosed us through the traffic home to Gullane House, commenting on the hot weather. The sun was still shining and life was going on in spite of what I'd just done.

Back at the estate, our neighbour carried my suitcase all the way up to our maisonette. There the ritual of tea-making could not dispel the awkwardness we all felt. Perhaps I was turning into my mother, but I didn't want this man, or even her, to make any mention of what had just happened. More than that, I didn't want anybody's pity. I excused myself and took my case upstairs to my room. I was tormented by the image of a nurse taking away the clothes I had bought for my daughter, and it cut me to the quick. What had happened to them? Had they been thrown away? Given to someone in greater need? I tried to rationalise. My little girl had another life now, and new clothes would be a part of that. Lots of beautiful new clothes.

My hand glided over a perfectly flat stomach. Somehow it had snapped miraculously back into place as though Sarah Louise had never been there. But I knew, and I would always know, that she had been. For nine months she had grown inside me and now she was missing.

I still had something to prove it. I opened my case and took out my toilet bag. Inside I found what I was looking for: a tiny plastic wrist tag with two words written on it – 'Baby Wassmer'.

I put it to my lips as the tears flowed. It was all I had left of her.

Chapter Seven

Afterbirth

For weeks after the birth I continued to hope that a photograph would arrive in the post. It never did. I cursed myself for not having taken one in the hospital but deep down I knew that an image captured at that time would only have preserved the moment of abandonment forever. A picture now, though – even a few weeks after our separation – a little piece of evidence that Sarah Louise was thriving in a new environment, might offer some justification, however small, for what I had done.

What I did get was a visit from a Home Office official. My mother was unnerved by this arrival on our doorstep, but the woman explained that she was simply gathering information for possible changes to the Adoption Act. It would all be completely confidential. My mother put the kettle on while I took this lady to my room. Sitting on the edge of my bed, she asked lots

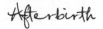

of questions, taking notes throughout our conversation. I assured her that I was fully aware of my rights. I knew I had six weeks from the birth before I had to sign the papers.

Years later I would learn that at the time the Adoption Act, which had been passed into law in 1958, was the subject of widespread criticism. A committee set up to examine its provisions was to report in 1972 recommending significant reform. This report became the basis for the Adoption Act of 1976, which repealed the 1958 legislation in its entirety. So I like to think my experience played some minuscule part in helping to improve the process for future mums.

In 1970, however, the adoption of my baby was being handled according to the old law. The Home Office lady had also brought with her a form she asked me to sign, provided I was happy to do so, for passport office paperwork that would allow the adoptive parents to take my baby on a short holiday abroad. In order to do this they needed my consent.

This request added another detail to my sketchy picture of this family's lifestyle. How wealthy they must be to be able to go off abroad. So far the only person in our family who had left these shores, except to fight in wars, was Aunt Carrie, who had been on a plane that did the 'loop de loop' while flying from Southend to Calais. And here was my baby travelling to a foreign country when she was only a few weeks old. It reinforced my conviction that Sarah Louise would have so many more opportunities with her new parents.

The days plodded by. The weather was still hot but the nights were getting longer. My parents never mentioned the concealed pregnancy or my baby's birth. The impending adoption, too, continued to be ignored. This avoidance of the issue was alienating me from them. I knew they must be wondering whether I was going to change my mind, but they never once asked me. Instead, they did their best to cheer me up, both taking a week's holiday from work even though we weren't going away anywhere. They simply stayed at home with me. I inferred from this that they believed I was doing the right thing and felt that now it was just a matter of getting me through it.

One day we went dog racing – all of us, even my mother. At the Wick my father made a fuss of me, buying me extra Russian salad. We were a family. I was their little girl again. But when I went to the ladies' and caught sight of myself in the mirror I noticed that my breasts were still leaking milk, staining the tie-dye dress I was wearing. I wasn't a little girl, I was a mother. A mother without a child.

I was also still Martin's girlfriend. Most evenings I walked to his flat, just as I'd always done. For the remainder of the summer I could be as carefree as the other young people singing along with Mungo Jerry. But I knew I was pretending, and everyone else knew it, too.

Carol and her husband had moved into the flat under Bridie's. Carol had recently given birth to her baby – a boy, like Hazel's – and I could hear him crying night and day. I was trying to behave as if nothing had happened. I was not prepared to accept pity from anyone, and especially not from other mothers. My head knew I had made the right decision but my body was still telling me otherwise, and I could not bring myself to hold this other baby. I felt numb when I looked out of the window one day to see Bridie in the garden, rocking back and forth as she cradled Carol's son tightly in her arms.

The documents were ready for signing. I was standing at a fork in the road with two clear paths before me. I could still choose motherhood. Martin believed it was too late, and I knew he was right. Strangers had now been taking care of my baby for far longer than I had. She had been with them for forty-two days; I'd shared only ten with her. I could not even imagine what Sarah Louise would look like by this time – not without a photograph. I still kept her wrist tag in my bedroom drawer but now, when I held it to my lips, I could no longer smell her sweet, baby scent. It had faded, as the words 'Baby Wassmer' were starting to do. She was someone else's child.

Nothing in my circumstances, or Martin's, had changed since we had first made our decision. Besides, everything was in motion, and although I knew that I could have pressed the button to stop the machinery,

I felt it would be irresponsible of me to do so at this late stage. The burden of our secret had been lifted from our shoulders and was being dealt with by important people – lawyers and courts and a host of other officials. If I dared change my mind now I would have been wrecking things for the new parents, who had stepped in to remedy my mistake. They were important people too, according to the JP. I had to stand fast.

I was no longer the feisty rebel of the Central Foundation School for Girls with her scorn for authority. I had been traumatised by an overwhelming sense of guilt stoked, as it turned out, by post-natal depression, and I wasn't the same girl any more. The experience had subdued me, robbed me of my teenagerhood. I'd seen the pain we had caused my mum and dad and Bridie. I felt I had ruined my parents' lives just when things had been looking up for them. Giving up Sarah Louise was, as it had always been, what I had to do to make things right.

I signed the documents.

In the autumn I got a job. I was now a junior librarian in the main branch library next door to the Whitechapel art gallery. I worked from nine to five most days and until 8pm one evening a week. Within a few months I had become an expert in the Dewey classification system and spent much of my time with my nose buried in the books that surrounded me.

I got on well with the rest of the staff and soon came to know the regular borrowers, who were mainly

students from Walbrook College on the Whitechapel Road, elderly men in search of large-print westerns by Zane Grey and permatanned Jewish ladies hankering after historical romance. Everyone else borrowed Mario Puzo's *The Godfather*, first published the previous year, which was still the library's most popular book by the end of 1970.

Away from the tranquillity of the library, however, I was a mess. My relationship with Martin was often fraught. When we met up in the evenings I tried to keep my emotions in check but I was liable to fly off the handle or sink into despair. We had both thought, naïvely, that once the baby had been adopted we could go back to normal. We were trying to carry on as if nothing had happened, but something *had* happened, something huge and life-changing. Although we had faced it together we hadn't been marked by it in the same way. I was the one who'd been through it; he was the one who had been waiting for me to come out the other side. I had been fundamentally changed by it; Martin hadn't. I bore the battle scars – stretch marks – to prove it.

On my way to Martin's house I often saw other girls heading towards the station at Mile End and a night out 'up West'. They looked about the same age as me but I knew that, inside and out, I was much older.

We had decided that I should go on the Pill and I had promised to go to the Brooke Advisory Centre, which provided free confidential advice on contraception to young people, but I kept putting it off. We didn't sleep together in six months. The truth was I didn't want to sleep with Martin, or anyone else. My mind and my body were resisting it because I knew to my cost what sex led to. How could I be a hundred per cent sure the Pill would be safe and it wouldn't happen again?

At home, we were on the phone at last. My mother bought a special telephone seat (Formica again) with a little padded cushion and a cupboard underneath for the directories. In an attempt to lighten my mood, she took photographs of me perched on it, the fashionable white receiver pressed to my ear, smiling emptily and talking to nobody, like a model in a cheesy advertisement. She was stealthily modifying my choice of decor and would eventually have the white sitting-room walls papered in a patterned design that totally ruined the effect of the white horse under the waterfall.

Meanwhile, I redecorated my own room, painting the walls matte black. If there were any doubt that I was suffering from post-natal depression, this ought to have been a clue. I completed the revamp with an Athena poster bearing the words of 'Desiderata' ('Go placidly amid the noise and haste…'), the ubiquitous New Age mantra of the times. King Crimson had used it to promote their album *Lizard* in 1970 and a recording of it by a US TV and radio host, Les Crane, backed by a gospel choir, was in the charts for four months in 1971. The line that most resonated with me was: 'And

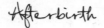

whether or not it is clear to you, no doubt the universe is unfolding as it should.'

My mother came home from work, looking forward to putting her feet up with a cigarette, took one look at my grim black room and exploded. 'You've done this on purpose, haven't you? Our lovely new flat and look what you've done!' She eventually got the council to repaper the walls.

I went to see Dr Teverson, who prescribed Librium. I took it for a while and then tried to do without it, but immediately I began to feel hollow, as if a hole had opened up inside me that would never be filled in. My baby's absence gnawed at me – an absence stronger than any presence. One night, consumed by loss, I wrote a poem as I struggled to make sense of it.

'Cuckoo'
Since you have gone,
Another shape now fills
The empty space between
The sheets.

It leaves no perfect mark
Upon the pillow.
At night, its silence
Breaks into my dreams,
With selfish screams it keeps me
From my sleep.

Tonight, it tries to suckle
On my soul,
This sullen, selfish stranger
To my womb.
And weakened by each silent breath it steals
I watch its shadow grow to fill my room.

Dr Teverson put me back on the Librium and signed me off work for a week while it began to take effect again. On my first day back, a kindly old deputy manager drew me to one side. He had seen the word 'depression' on my doctor's certificate. 'What's a lovely young girl like you got to be depressed about?' I wished I could tell him but I couldn't.

In the spring of 1971 we were joined by a new member of staff. Like Martin, David was a couple of years older than I was, tall, slim and wore his hair long. He was passionate about art, and one afternoon I went with him next door to the Whitechapel gallery. As we wandered around the canvases his appreciation of and enthusiasm for the paintings opened my eyes to a world I had not explored much beyond the pages of *The Book of Knowledge.* Soon we were going to other exhibitions, taking in bold images by Gilbert and George, and David Hockney; to the Tate gallery and the Courtauld Institute. One afternoon, looking at some Post-Impressionist paintings by Bonnard, I began to understand how life – maybe even my own life – could be viewed from new perspectives.

It wasn't long before I was checking the library timesheets to see when David and I would be scheduled to work together. I started to look forward to his company. I started to look forward, period.

Martin and I were drifting apart. Now, when I went round to his flat in the evenings, he would doze on the sofa, tired out after working on a building site every day. I would be left sitting beside him watching television. We had, it seemed, nothing left to say to each other. We had been through too much, too soon. We both knew that we could never have coped with our baby, but it was clear that we couldn't cope with the loss of our baby, either. We had persevered for over a year since Sarah Louise's birth, handling the grief in our own ways, and we had moved on – but apart, not together. It was as if we'd become different people.

When we broke up, in July 1971, it was not with a bang but a whimper. One night I just decided not to visit him. I called him on the phone and he didn't argue. He told me he was busy, too. We let each other be and when we met again a few weeks later, things felt better between us. We had given each other permission to pursue our respective new lives.

By the end of August I was officially going out with David. Initially I'd wanted to keep him separate from my life at home, just as I'd done with Martin, but David was a different character altogether, outgoing and upbeat, and he wasn't having any of that. He just turned up at Gullane House and introduced himself to my mum and dad.

My parents were pleased about this new relationship. For them it drew a line under the past. And they loved David. He talked politics with my father and charmed my mother. He even appreciated her kitsch knick-knacks, laughing with her over 'Apron pink – weather stink!'. David was good for me, too. He was a positive person, always looking forward rather than back. I had told him about Sarah Louise and the adoption and he had taken it all in his stride. He offered me a way out of the maze of dark days towards a possibility of brighter times I couldn't have envisaged a few months earlier and his infectious passion for art was helping me to broaden my mind again. I loved him perhaps even more than I'd loved Martin. I was no longer taking anti-depressants.

David moved into a flat in Wimbledon, sharing with a friend, and I spent a lot of time with him there. Compared with the East End it was like being in the countryside and we enjoyed long walks across Wimbledon Common. At home, he stretched canvases and painted me. I was flattered to be his muse.

With my life slowly getting back on an even keel, I realised that to even begin to justify the agony of having Sarah Louise adopted, I needed to work towards a better future for myself as well as for her. The first step was to make up for my abandoned education. Encouraged by David, I put in my notice at the library

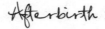

and enrolled at Walbrook College just down the road to begin studying that autumn for the A-Levels I'd missed.

The course was only a year long but I hoped, by the end of it, to have gained passes in English and history. I expected to do better in English, my strongest subject – but that was before I knew that one of my history tutors would be John Merrington, a charismatic Western Marxist historian who went on to write for the *New Left Review* and to publish several highly respected books. No teacher could have been more of an inspiration, even if his coverage could be a little lopsided. I recall spending months on the French Revolution and then rattling through several less interesting and uncontroversial periods at great speed.

A whiff of rebellion remained in the air after the events of 1968 and clearly it still motivated John. So as well as learning about the storming of the Bastille and the fall of the Ancien Régime, we were treated to updates on strikes at European car plants. Like all good teachers, he considered himself to be a student, too, and apart from being brilliant at his subject he was funny, irreverent and always 'one of us'.

A year later, I had my two A-Level passes: a B in English but an A for history – as, I assume, did all John's other students. David, meanwhile, had won a place at Wimbledon School of Art. It wasn't all plain sailing by any means, but we were going forward together.

The first hiccup had come in the summer of 1972, immediately after I sat my final exam. I took off to the pub to celebrate with a group of fellow students and, in a moment of madness, accepted an invitation to head straight off for a weekend jaunt in the Hampshire countryside. There I ended up having a brief fling with another student from my English course. Maybe it was a kind of emotional altitude sickness after ascending from the depths of despair to the exhilaration of having finished college; maybe I was subconsciously trying to recapture the chunk of my teenage years I felt I'd missed out on. Whatever the reason, David was deeply upset and my dad, feeling for him, took him off dog racing to try to cheer him up.

Once I'd recovered my equilibrium we patched things up, and when David started his foundation course at art school we set up home together in a rented flat in Wimbledon. He wasn't awarded a grant for the foundation course so I did a variety of short-term jobs to support us financially – bar work, temping for an agency in central London and even the odd spell as an artists' model at the art school.

Times were tough and there were a lot of people on the dole searching for work. Only two weeks after Sarah Louise's birth in 1970, the Conservatives had returned to power under Edward Heath and had set about trying to rein in the unions. Since then there had been massive inflation, pay restraints and high unemployment. War in the Middle East sent oil prices

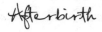

rocketing and there were strikes by everyone, it seemed, from civil servants to London dockers. Most significant were two mineworkers' strikes over pay.

My father was still fighting to save the Royal Mint from being moved to Llantrisant. By this time he was spending more time at Westminster than he was at the Mint, and counted several Labour MPs as his friends. Outraged and appalled by the government's unwilling-ness to negotiate, he was encouraged by the strong popular support for the miners, which he saw as a good omen for his own cause.

In the New Year of 1974, in an attempt to conserve fuel resources, the government introduced the infamous three-day week. People had to work by lamplight or candlelight, if they were able to work at all, govern-ment ministers advised us to take baths in the dark, there was a 50mph speed restriction on all roads and the television regularly shut down at 10pm. David and I dampened stale bread and reheated it in the oven. It was what I imagined wartime austerity to have been like.

On the eve of my twenty-first birthday we were staying with my parents. It wasn't much of a celebra-tion as I'd ended up in bed with 'flu. My father brought me soup. He wasn't well, either: he had a stomach upset. After a few days I was better but he was much worse. He was in a great deal of pain and could not keep any food down. He believed he suffered from gastric ulcers but he had little faith in the ability of the medical profession to cure them. It was clear to my mother and me that the stress and uncertainty of the situation at the Mint might well have aggravated my dad's condition but he was too scared to see the doctor. He had watched an uncle of his develop stomach cancer and was haunted by a vivid memory of visiting him in hospital in his final days. Scanning the ward for the robust man he knew, my father had been horrified to see something resembling a shrivelled monkey in his place.

My father was finally persuaded to see Dr Teverson, who recommended hospital tests. I was at work, temping in London, when I got a call from my mother. At the hospital, a doctor had informed her it was cancer. She hadn't told my father and could not contemplate doing so. I understood exactly how she felt. Relying on my old friend denial, I convinced myself that he would pull through. My mother was equally convinced that he wasn't going to survive. I knew she was haunted by her own ghost: her dead brother, Johnny.

We told my father that he had an ulcer that required surgery. He was apprehensive about the operation but relieved to be having the problem attended to at last. He was even more relieved not to be hearing that it was cancer. He recovered quickly, declaring that he felt like a new man.

In the meantime, Ted Heath had called a snap election and had been defeated, leaving Harold Wilson to lead a minority Labour administration. When Wilson

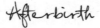

accepted a pay board's recommendation to award the miners an 'exceptional' pay rise and agreed to invest in new coalfields, my dad was grimly satisfied. There was to be no good news in his own battle with the government, however. The closure of the Mint at Tower Hill was by now irrevocable: the transfer to South Wales was on course to be completed by the end of the following year.

My mum refused to even consider relocating to Wales. She had been evacuated to Fishguard during the war as a teenager and had been so homesick she had run away and returned to the East End to dodge the bombs with her mother. She would never cope with living away from London. But I knew my father would not cope with empty days. He had worked all his life and lived for his work. What on earth would he do without it?

For now he took time off to convalesce and he and my mother started to get out and about in a way they hadn't done for years, taking trips to Goodwood races and coach excursions to the seaside. In the background, the spectre of redundancy was looming.

One morning at Gullane House, I hear him retching in the toilet. The cancer is back.

Chapter Eight

The Road Out

Although we never spoke of it, my father must have known he was dying. Just as I had done when I was pregnant, he put off going into hospital for as long as he could. Like father, like daughter. But in his case there was a crucial difference: he was in no doubt that once he went in he would never come out.

Eventually Dr Teverson admitted him to Homerton Hospital. The Salvation Army Mothers' Hospital, where I had given birth, had since been assimilated into Homerton. The place where Sarah Louise had entered the world was to be the same place from which my father would leave it.

During his last weeks he grew weak and was in constant pain. Having been a cheerful optimist all his life, he was now not only scared but dogged by depression. The workers at the Mint were being laid off and a friend came in to visit bringing papers for him to sign so that he wouldn't lose out on a redundancy package. Everything was failing him: the Mint, his health and perhaps me, too. When I was sitting at his bedside one day he asked me to place my hands on his stomach. It was as if he believed I could heal him with my love. I leaned closer, spreading out my fingers across his abdomen. We never talked about the cancer growing in his belly or the baby that had grown in mine. He confessed only that he was irritable when visitors came and lonely when they didn't.

When the doctors administered morphine he was euphoric. With the pain suddenly alleviated, he thought he had been cured. When he learned that the improvement was down to drugs, he felt cheated. Now he began to deliver warnings: I should give up smoking, I must never take drugs, I should find a man to take good care of me. This last command was a clear criticism of David.

It was now the autumn of 1974. In the summer David and I had bought a tiny flat in Wimbledon, which we could just about afford with the aid of a council mortgage. David, having completed his foundation course, was about to start his fine arts degree. From September he would be on a full mature student's grant – and so would I. The casual work I'd taken on to support us wasn't exactly fulfilling and, feeling that my life was losing momentum and my mind was beginning to stagnate, I had successfully applied for and won a place to study for an honours degree in English and history at Kingston Polytechnic in Surrey. I relished the prospect of being able to lose myself in books for three whole years.

Over the summer I had been spending a lot of time with my parents as my dad's condition began to deteriorate. David and I had seen little of each other. But it had not escaped my notice that he was growing close to a girl from his foundation course. He always seemed too busy to visit my father and my parents sensed that something was wrong. It was clear to me that I was unwillingly becoming a corner of some kind of love triangle, but both David and his girlfriend kept insisting their relationship was platonic. We muddled on through the summer, with David absent most days but still technically living at home, until finally I was confronted with incontrovertible evidence that he was being unfaithful.

I was hardly in position to cast the first stone, having briefly gone off the rails myself a couple of years earlier. This, however, was more than a fling: my boyfriend was in love, but not with me. I should have been heartbroken but my father's illness put the fact that I was losing my partner into perspective. David was still alive and well, whereas my dad, the only constant male presence in my life, would soon be gone forever. There was no doubt in my mind as to where my priorities lay. The knowledge that my partner was involved with someone else, though upsetting, was not insurmountable. What did hurt me, and indeed made me feel utterly betrayed, was the deceit. And his timing was rotten, too.

I made an appointment with a doctor in Wimbledon who prescribed Valium. It took the edge off my jagged emotions and gave me the confidence to do what I had decided I must do. I packed up David's things, rang him at his new girlfriend's flat and told him that if he had any feelings left for me at all, he should collect his belongings and move out.

In the end it was a civilised split, thanks to a doctor's prescription. With hindsight, I know that I made the right decision in bringing matters to a head because David's relationship with his girlfriend turned out to be a significant one: they went on to have children and were to stay together for almost twenty years.

My mother, on the other hand, was unable to accept what she saw as David's desertion. One evening when I was at Gullane House she phoned him at his girlfriend's flat and begged him to come home to me. He explained that he couldn't, but she carried on relentlessly trying to persuade him. I listened from the kitchen, eyes tight shut, vowing that never again would I trust a man to catch me when I fell.

So when I started college that September, I did so as a twenty-one-year-old singleton. I had been there only a matter of weeks when I had a late-night call in Wimbledon from the hospital to say that my father was fading fast. My mother was already at his bedside and I should have left home immediately, but instead I stalled for time, waiting for the morning light and hoping to be spared another goodbye in a hospital ward. I was. By the time I arrived, it was too late for words.

I left my mother sitting in a corridor while I went into my father's ward. The curtains around his bed were drawn but through a gap I could see doctors pounding on his chest, trying in vain to restart his heart. His mouth was open and the life was running out of him. I ran out too, back to the corridor, where my mother registered the terrible shock in my face. She, of all people, knew how obstinately I had been hiding from the truth, hoping against hope that by some miracle my father would survive. By now we were both world authorities on denial.

We went home in a minicab. At some point in our journey a gentle reggae song by Ken Boothe began playing on the driver's radio.

> ... *And I would give anything I own,*
> *Give up my life, my heart, my home.*
> *I would give anything I own,*
> *Just to have you back again.*

My mother started to sob quietly beside me. This time, as I took her hand in mine, it was my turn to say, 'Don't cry.'

After my father's death, I took to spending every weekend with my mother. I managed to suppress my grief over the double loss of my partner and my father

– or suppress it enough to be able to function normally. I took sanctuary at college, just as I had at the library after I'd given up my baby for adoption, immersing myself in my studies while I recovered, knowing that here I didn't have to explain anything to anyone. I was just another student working hard for her degree.

My mother, however, wasn't coping on her own. She still had her job at the coffee house but she would return at night to an empty home and drink three bottles of Guinness to help her sleep. Gradually she developed the habit of adding nips of vodka or brandy. Alcohol was becoming her refuge, just as the pub had been all those years earlier. Now, though, she didn't seem to go out anywhere except to work and the hairdresser's. Increasingly, she began to live her life vicariously through mine.

She gave me £2,000 of the money my dad had left her – most of which must have consisted of his redundancy compensation from the Mint – to assist me in holding on to the Wimbledon flat. Even so, with the whole mortgage to pay on my own I still needed to work to supplement my grant. As I had to keep weekends free for my mother, I got an evening bar job.

Not long after my father died, we heard that he was to be awarded the British Empire Medal. My mother and I were invited to tea at 11 Downing Street to receive it on his behalf from the latest chancellor of the exchequer, Denis Healey, who sent a smart car to collect us from her council flat. Had my father been alive it might have been quite an occasion. Although he had never been one for pomp or titles (and leaving aside his feelings about what had happened to the Mint), I think he would have allowed himself a little pride at having been recognised for his loyal service to the institution and to his fellow workers. He might also have been keen to take a quick shufti round the chancellor's quarters.

During his struggle to keep the Mint at Tower Hill, my father would not have dealt much with Denis Healey, if at all, as by the time Healey took office in the Wilson government elected in 1974, my dad was already ill. Evidently the chancellor had not been properly briefed about the recipient of the medal because he put his foot in it straight away by asking why Mr Wassmer had been unable to make it that day. If my father had been alive my mother would have been chuffed to have entered 11 Downing Street on his arm. But her grief was still too raw and her reaction to the chancellor's mistake was bitter. She dropped her usual deference to her 'betters', filled him in on his error and proceeded to berate him about the high mortgage rate I was paying.

The last coin to come out of Tower Hill, a gold sovereign, would be struck in November 1975 – almost exactly a year after my father's death. It was the end of an era.

Meanwhile, my dad's sister, Aunt Joan, and her husband Fred came to visit my mother, bringing a stranger with them, an elderly lady. I stood up quickly as my mum showed her into the sitting room and introduced her to me. 'This is Lil. Your grandmother.'

At long last Lil Wassmer, née Tolliday, was standing in front of me – short, plump and dressed in a black coat with a bright paste brooch on the lapel. I scanned her face, searching for similarities between us. I could detect only one: she had the same dark, curly hair I had struggled to straighten as a teenager, though as she must have been eighty years old by this time, she may have needed a little help with the colour these days. I could see she was the woman I remembered from a small black-and-white photograph I had once glued into an album. It showed my father as a young man, sitting on a country fence with his mother standing beside him. It had been taken on a working holiday they had spent together picking hops in Kent. In the picture my father wears a short-sleeved shirt, unbuttoned at the neck. Suntanned and healthy, he smiles for the camera. Lil's arm is behind him, possibly holding him, a warm palm pressed against his back. They are close, not just physically, but tied by the bonds of blood and love. What caused them to break those bonds? And perhaps more important, what was it that prevented them from ever being reconciled?

Lil took off her coat and sat down on the sofa beside me, accepting tea from my mother. I wanted to ask about an argument over the cooking of roast beef but my mum was chatting nervously, filling the conversational gaps created by my father's absence. Did Lil know I was studying for an honours degree? Did she know that Billy had received a posthumous honour which had been presented to us at Downing Street by Denis Healey?

As my mother talked, my grandmother looked at me sitting there beside her. Perhaps now it was her turn to search my face for evidence of herself or her Billy. But I was a stranger, too. Her son was gone and we all knew it was too late for them to be reunited.

I spoke up and told Lil about the day we had all gone to visit her. She glanced at my mother, as though seeking confirmation.

'It's true,' my mother said.

I explained how, on that rainy afternoon, we had stood on Lil's front doorstep. As I recounted the story, I had an image in mind of my father lighting damp cigarettes with nervous fingers. Lil thought for a moment. 'I would've been at Joan's,' she decided. 'I was there most weekends.'

She didn't ask why we hadn't come again or why we had never mentioned our abortive visit to Aunt Joan. An almost reverential hush descended on the room as if everyone was privately mourning a lost opportunity.

My mother stood up and went into the kitchen to make more tea. Lil stared down at tense fingers. The blood that ran through her veined hands was the same as mine, and I was considering something else we had in common: we were both mothers who had lost our children. I kept that to myself. And my mum, returning now with fresh tea, did the same.

At the front door we promised to keep in touch but although Lil was to live for another five years it didn't happen. Perhaps we had been estranged for too long, and the connection was just too tenuous, with my father gone, for any of us to make the effort to maintain it. I never saw my grandmother again.

More lost opportunities. I consoled myself with the thought that, while it was too late for Lil Wassmer to be reconciled with her lost child, I still had a future ahead of me, and in that future rested the chance that I might one day be reunited with mine.

Having had my fingers burned by my relationship with David, I was keen to steer well clear of romantic entanglements for a while. I had a circle of good friends in Wimbledon, established over the years I'd spent there since first meeting David, and, though my flat was tiny, I now had my own space. I also had a surrogate family. My close friend Maria was the mother of three small daughters, Debbie, Lizzie and Kate. After Kate's arrival in 1972 they had all been christened in one ceremony, in which I had stood godmother to the three of them.

Seeing the girls almost daily, I witnessed the milestones and landmarks of their young lives, listening to Debbie reading aloud from a favourite storybook, sharing the pleasure of Kate's first steps and words. Lizzie, just four months younger than my own daughter, was in particular a constant reminder of how Sarah Louise would be growing and developing. Maria was the most beautiful and most generous woman I would ever meet. She was half Chinese and half Portuguese, an orphan from Macao brought to England as a baby to live with foster parents. She'd had a tough childhood and still needed a proper family. I was a part of it. When she went on to have two more children, Joe and Suzie, I became their godmother, too.

Yet in many ways my function in my goddaughters' world in the mid-1970s was more older sibling than surrogate mum. In an echo of my years as the class clown, I assumed the role of mad auntie and played it to the hilt. I resisted behaving too maternally with all children. I had put the adoption behind me now and had moved on in perhaps every way but one: with the passing years, I was becoming increasingly certain that I could not contemplate the idea of having more children myself.

In the Children Act of 1975 and the new Adoption Act of 1976, adopted people over the age of eighteen were given the right to apply for their original birth certificate. Under the changes to the Adoption Act, they were also able to go to the courts for information about the agency and local authority involved in their adoption. While I nurtured the hope that once she reached eighteen Sarah Louise would come looking for me, I could not bear the thought that she might knock on my door one day to discover me with other children. How would I find the words to explain how one child could be kept and another abandoned?

A more recently acquired friend was Mark, a guitarist who had just dropped out of an architecture course at Kingston Poly. Mark was six-foot-four and so good-looking that my friend Theresa dubbed him Goldenballs on first sight, decades before Posh told the world it was her nickname for Becks. Mark was handsome all right, but he was a best buddy, not a boyfriend. He was charming, witty and talented – and married to his music. He played reggae and funk almost every night in a popular London band called the Strutters. He was on the dole, I was scraping by on my grant and meagre barmaid's wages so money was tight, but we had great fun together, and plenty of adventures, driving around the city from one music venue to another in a classic Volkswagen convertible that needed pushing almost everywhere we went.

Mark was living in an overcrowded college flat share at the end of my street. As the weeks went by, he began to spend more time at my place than in his own. Late at night, I'd hear the familiar rumble of his car engine arriving outside after band rehearsals. It wasn't long before he had taken up residence, slowly but steadily having transferred his few possessions from the flat down the road to mine. I wasn't complaining. I loved his company. Besides, I was with my mother at weekends and during the week I spent most of my free time with Mark anyway. It would be a temporary arrangement, he said. He ended up staying for nine years.

Studying for my degree, doing my bar job, going around with Mark's band and sharing my life with my mother was something of a juggling act, and from time to time I dropped the balls. One day my college tutor tackled me for not working hard enough and I was forced to come clean. I explained that I was having trouble keeping up as I needed to supplement my grant with evening shifts in a bar in order to meet my mortgage payments. When my tutor suggested I tried switching to weekend shifts I had to tell her I went home then to be with my widowed mother. I had no choice but to knuckle down, and in the end I got there, gaining my degree in the summer of 1977.

On graduation day, I saw my mum sitting proudly among the other parents. I also saw the space beside her where my father should have been. Posing for the customary photograph in mortar board and gown, clutching a scroll in my left hand, I smiled for the camera. But inside I felt torn. I wondered why I hadn't done this while my father was alive to see it. Why was it always so important to me to go my own way? I didn't have an answer. All I had was the sense that I was constantly searching for the right path, for a road that might take me to the life I felt was out there somewhere. The life I should be leading. Aimless as it was, I couldn't deviate from that quest.

Chapter Nine

Into the Westy

I had my degree, but I didn't have a clue what to do with it, or what to do next. I found myself writing short stories, some of which were published in the free magazines aimed at young women that were handed out at tube stations in those days, consisting mainly of ads for secretarial jobs and flat shares. But they were never going to pay the mortgage, and I didn't have enough success to give me the confidence to believe I could make a living out of writing. Mark was moving on with his music, now fronting a new-wave band called the Sinceros, but earning very little from it. So we were struggling and constantly on the look-out for schemes that would give us the chance to make what we called 'easy money', though it was rarely easy and sometimes not even money.

One evening I was cooking while Mark was telling me some news about a mutual friend, Paul, who worked for a record company that re-released old blues and soul records. Apparently, Paul was organising a morale-boosting convention for his sales team and had the idea that some form of musical interlude, complete with floor show, might grab the reps' attention and spur them on to achieve greater targets. He had decided that Nina Simone's 'I Put a Spell on You' fitted the bill perfectly. He'd told Mark that he now needed someone to play the part of a red devil, who would enter the conference room in a cloud of swirling smoke to perform a spellbinding dance and then pin a promotional badge on the lapel of each sales rep. Unfortunately, Paul's budget didn't run to the cost of hiring a professional entertainer.

I stirred my casserole, only half-listening to this story, which had nothing much to do with me. Mark leaned closer. Wait till I heard exactly how much Paul's budget was. A hundred pounds. Didn't I think that might go a very long way in the hands of two broke young people with the initials M and J?

I looked at Mark and saw his smile. The penny dropped. Me? A red devil? It was an absurd, if not outrageous, proposition. I thought about it a little more. Maybe if Paul could stretch to £150, we'd have a deal.

A few days later Paul called me to confirm a few details. We would get half our fee up front. The day before my performance, the company's head of sales promotions was to accompany me to a theatrical hire store, where he would take care of the cost of an impressive costume. Mark would be responsible for transport, as well as the hire and operation of a smoke machine. I duly met up with Rob, a young northerner sporting shoulder-length hair and a mouthful of chewing gum, outside a famous costume-hire store in North London. As he looked me up and down it was clear he wasn't totally convinced of my suitability for this inspirational piece of theatre, but, there again, the right outfit might help.

Rob explained to the store assistant what we required and a selection was duly made. I took an outfit into a changing cubicle while Rob waited for me outside. As I pulled the costume out of its protective bag my heart began to sink. It wasn't even red, more a faded orange – and bri-nylon to boot. I got into it to discover it was far too large and bagged unflatteringly around the bottom and crotch. I tried on the *pièce de résistance*, the accompanying headpiece, and checked the result in the cubicle mirror. Two knitted horns on my skull were facing east and west.

When I came out of the cubicle, Rob stopped chewing his gum and his jaw dropped open. 'No way,' he protested to the store assistant. 'You're going to have to do better than that. We're supposed to be a top-class record company!'

It took a while to find another outfit that was any more suitable but we were running out of time and eventually we opted for the best of a bad bunch. Rob paid the deposit and fee and we parted company. Back at my flat, I put on my costume again and stood in front of a mirror trying out various demonic poses. At that moment, Mark arrived home, carrying something that resembled a portable heater. This, I learned, was the smoke machine. He studied me from all angles. Ever the perfectionist, he suggested I might try to lose half a stone overnight.

The next morning we set off in the Volkswagen. It was a clear, sunny day so we took down the roof and made our way to a depressingly soulless motel on the M1. There we discovered that Paul had coerced a colleague into lending his two small children for the occasion, a boy and a girl aged between about five and seven. They had been painted green and were dressed as imps. Paul, a cool character at the best of times, was uncharacteristically animated.

'Right. So you'll burst in with the kids either side of you, sort of sheltering under your cape as you do the dance. Got it?'

'Got it.'

In a dressing room, I changed into my outfit, loading on plenty of thick make-up to make sure I would never be recognised by any member of my audience should our paths cross again. Then I went downstairs with my imps.

I found Mark in the hallway, outside the door to the conference room. He was setting up the smoke machine.

'Remind me again why we're doing this?' I was losing confidence with each second that passed.

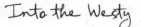

'Easy money,' Mark replied. He offered me an encouraging smile. 'Cheer up. It'll all be over in a few minutes. Just wait for the music, then I'll switch on the machine and you go in and do your bit. Those reps probably won't even see you as the room'll be full of smoke.'

I managed to raise a smile now. He was right. It was easy money.

The first few bars of 'I Put a Spell on You' struck up on the other side of the door. Everyone sprang into action. I gathered the imps under my cape and Mark pressed the button on his machine. In a matter of seconds we were all engulfed by smoke. 'Go!' said Mark. I leaned forward, searching blindly for the door handle. Having found it, I turned and pulled it but the door wouldn't open. I couldn't see a thing. Nor could anyone else. Then a loud fire alarm began to sound. The imps screamed in fright and took off back down the hallway.

'Come back!' I yelled, but they were long gone. Nina Simone was still singing on the other side of the door.

'Go *on*!' urged Mark.

I struggled with the door handle again.

'It won't open!' I hissed, still trying to pull it.

Mark pushed instead and the door finally flew open in front of me. As I entered the room, a single puff of smoke followed me before being extinguished as the fire door swung shut on heavy hinges. After a few fumbled attempts to prop it open, Mark gave up and it closed behind me.

I was standing in a huge convention room. On a stage, Paul sat with Rob and some other record company officials. I offered him a limp smile but he showed no spark of recognition, giving only a slight jerk of his head as if to remind me what I was being paid for. As Nina continued to sing, I threw myself around the room, cavorting among several rows of sales reps. Some looked bemused, others embarrassed as I pinned, with shaking fingers, small badges to their lapels. As the record finally stopped playing, my imps showed up at last and stood uncertainly on either side of me. I took a bow, but Paul's head was in his hands.

Rather than return to the dressing room, Mark decided it might be better if we just left the building. I wasn't going to argue. Still wearing my costume, I hurried through the hotel towards the car park, leaving Mark calling after me that he'd catch me up once he had talked to Paul and Rob. Aeons passed before he appeared. In the meantime numerous hotel guests came over to point and gawp at the red devil seated in the passenger seat of an ancient VW convertible. When Mark finally arrived, he quickly turned the key in the ignition and we sped off, racing as quickly as possible back down the motorway.

'What took you so long?' I groaned.

'I wanted to get the rest of the money.'

'Where is it?'

Mark ran his hand through his hair, something he always did when he was anxious. There was a slight grimace of unease on his face.

'Rob forgot his chequebook,' he said. 'But he swears he'll post it to us on Monday.'

A lorry honked loudly as it passed us. It sounded very much like a burst of laughter, which was appropriate, considering that the promised cheque never did arrive. Instead, after paying for the hire of a smoke machine and petrol – we were each about a tenner up. Easy money indeed.

Not surprisingly, I was eventually forced to go on the dole. After a few months went by with no sign of me getting a proper job I was offered 'suitable employment'. It was an offer I couldn't refuse as it came accompanied by a warning that turning it down could result in my benefit being stopped. I was obliged to become the roundest peg in the squarest of holes: a clerical officer at my local Social Security office.

At my new workplace, mired in benefit rates, assessments and guidelines, I found I had less in common with my fellow employees than I did with the claimants on the other side of the counter. It appeared to me that most of the staff felt the power they wielded over the finances of others gave them a licence to treat hard-up claimants with contempt, and in some cases you'd have thought the money was coming out of their own pockets. I seemed to be the only one who actually preferred sitting on reception, dealing with people, rather than fiddling with forms and calculations back in the office.

The option of flexitime, which enabled me to start work late at 10am and leave early at 3pm, was my salvation – but only until the last week of the month, when I would have to make up my full quota of hours. That week was like a prison sentence. If I had committed a crime, I reflected ruefully after my escape, I might have served less time than the two years I ended up spending at the Social Security office.

The staff were expected to participate in various extra-curricular activities, presumably designed to motivate us, bond us and perhaps to relieve the tedium of our jobs. This depressing period was enlivened for me only by the area office drama tournament, in which we won a trophy – the Silver Rose Bowl – for our entry, a play called *The Waiting Room* in which I took the role of a crazy old lady who sat there the entire time knitting a large, unrecognisable item of clothing. Years later I was to use the whole unhappy experience of working at the Social Security office in a play of my own, *One of Us*, about an out-of-work actor press-ganged into the civil service to help win his boss a coveted drama prize.

In the summer of 1979 I was finally sprung from jail by a request to tender my resignation for the cardinal sin of absconding from the field on our annual sports day, an event for which there had been a tacit three-line whip.

Once liberated, I quickly signed up for a secretarial course to increase my job options and avoid having to become a 'claimant' all over again. I soon learned to type with ten fingers instead of my usual two, and began to master Pitman's shorthand, though not before dismaying my teacher with some atrocious errors in translation. I managed to read 'balance sheet' as 'bullshit', thanked a fictional company for 'apricots' rather than 'products' and described a man 'peering behind a hedge' as 'peeing'. Despite my shortcomings, I qualified and managed to get a secretarial job working in a BBC Radio outpost called Transcription Services in Shepherd's Bush.

The main role of this department was to update and edit radio programmes for transmission overseas, taking out contemporary references that were too English to mean anything to people in, say African countries, though some original programmes were made, too, including a radio version of *Top of the Pops*. I was secretary to a group of producers in the fields of light entertainment, classical music and drama, all areas which interested me.

It wasn't long before one of my bosses approached me to ask if I would do him a favour: though it wasn't part of my job, he wondered if I could possibly write a publicity blurb for *The Goon Show*, an old series, slightly rejigged, that was being sent round the world. I was hardly going to complain about spending an afternoon listening to a comedy programme I'd enjoyed with my parents as a young kid. In no time I was doing most of my boss's comedy publicity – actually being paid to chuckle away in an empty office to the likes of Tony Hancock. The wages weren't great but I enjoyed what I was doing and the department was lively. It also had a subsidised bar, which may have been a factor in my remaining there for nearly four and a half years.

For Mark, success was proving elusive. In spite of securing a record deal with CBS, completing a US tour and releasing three well-received albums, the Sinceros still hadn't had a hit. Although he was still being encouraged by the CBS executives to stick with it, he was beginning to consider throwing in the towel. On one occasion, the head of A&R tipped him off that a rhythm guitarist was being sought by a band he was certain had huge potential. They were due to play at Nelson's, a music club on the premises of Wimbledon Football Club. It was suggested he should go along and check them out.

He was back home within half an hour, long before the end of the set.

'Any good?' I asked, though I could tell from his early return and morose expression that this was unlikely.

'Rubbish,' he said. 'They'll never get anywhere.' He went to the fridge for a can of beer. 'In fact, the best I can say is that they're very aptly named.'

The band was called Dire Straits.

One evening I was sitting with Mark in a local pub, trying my hardest to lift his spirits and persuade him not to give up. 'You've got a record deal, contacts, talent – don't waste it all. Just keep going and you'll make a breakthrough eventually.' I was beginning to sound like my father.

Mark wasn't impressed. 'If you think it's so easy,' he said, 'you try.' Over a few more drinks an idea came to us.

A few months later, in spite of being unable to sing, I had recorded a single, produced by Mark, which he had somehow managed to sell to Epic, a subsidiary of CBS. I had added lyrics to a hand-clapping tune sung by kids in playgrounds, entitled it 'The Schoolgirl Song' and performed it under the pseudonym Lola Payola.

The head of A&R said he had never heard anything quite like it. I didn't doubt him for a minute. But he took the tape home and played it to his kids, who instantly recognised the tune and loved the record. That got him thinking it might just prove to be a 'bullet'. On the strength of that instinct he offered us a three-album production deal.

There was just one tiny snag. My alter-ego, Lola Payola, was supposed to be a schoolgirl whereas I was a twenty-eight-year-old office worker. Well, two snags: I wasn't a teenager and I couldn't sing. If it did turn out to be a hit, we were going to have a problem appearing on *Top of the Pops*, something all British bands with a single in the charts would be required by their record companies to do. Mark insisted on an opt-out clause in the contract. CBS were shocked. Apparently, only one other band had ever refused to do *Top of the Pops* – the politically aware Clash, and their decision had been ideologically credible – but in the end CBS agreed to this stipulation and Lola's single was released.

Although the late, lamented DJ John Peel, famous for promoting new artists, regularly played 'The School-girl Song' on his highly respected Radio One show, it soon became clear that I had absolutely no reason to fear being exposed as requests for public appearances were not exactly pouring into the CBS office. The record, described by one local-radio DJ as 'weird but pointless', soon sank without trace. Apart from a few royalties that continued to trickle in from (of all places) Finland, it made very little money. Mark and I failed to produce a follow-up single, thus breaking our contract with the record company.

When I told my mother about the record she didn't seem to believe me. I had to show her the carefully posed photograph of me on the record sleeve to convince her. Then she simply stared at me, slightly bemused, as though I was playing a practical joke on her.

I was still visiting her every weekend, still trying to get her interested in life beyond Gullane House and the coffee shop. I offered to take her to an ice-dancing show. She liked to watch ice-skating on television and knew the names of all the stars – Robin Cousins, John Curry, Torvill and Dean. But she declined. The theatre was bound to be cold with all that ice, she said. Much better to view it in comfort at home.

One night we were sitting in front of the television, watching an old film we had enjoyed together many times, Hitchcock's *Rebecca*. It was coming to its conclusion as the naïve and unconfident young wife, played by Joan Fontaine, plucks up the courage to tackle the difficult subject of her husband's ex, Rebecca – the woman to whom Fontaine's character felt she never matched up.

I looked across at my mother, cigarette poised between her trembling fingers, a tall glass of Guinness beside her on the coffee table I had chosen all those years before. I braced myself and decided to tackle a difficult subject of my own that had dogged me since childhood.

'The certificate …' I began.

My mum glanced over at me but her attention was still on the film.

'The wedding certificate, for you and Dad. Who was "the divorced wife of George Townsend"?'

She concentrated on the television for a moment and then looked back at me again. I knew she was wondering why I was asking this now.

'It was you, wasn't it?' I prompted.

Eventually, she nodded.

'Why didn't you tell me?'

She gave a small shrug. 'It didn't seem important. Just something that happened a long time ago. When I was young.'

Could it be that we were at long last managing to talk to one another? Not about food or shopping or the neighbours or an article in a magazine, but really talking, about something important? She took another sip of her drink. A mystery began to unravel. As a girl, she had met a man and fallen in love. First love. Just like Martin and me. She and George Townsend had married and moved to a big house in Essex. They even had their own piano. She'd had everything she ever wanted, including George's love, until she realised her own feelings were not love but infatuation. She knew she had made a mistake so she had run home to her mother in Cable Street, Stepney, and become the divorced wife of George Townsend.

Essex. Perhaps that's why my father had hated it so much: my mother had once belonged to someone else there. All those years we had struggled in two poky rooms beneath a rain-sodden roof, she and my father had lived with the knowledge of what she had given up for true love.

'I always knew it was you,' I said.

'I know. But what's done is done.'

What's done is done. For one evening, my mother and I were able to dismantle the wall between us and have the beginnings of a proper conversation, but soon she was retreating into herself once more. Nothing in

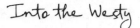

the real world seemed to live up to the one she inhab-
ited in her imagination. Sometimes, when she'd had a
little too much to drink, she would say, 'I wonder what
happened to your baby?' She never said it without a
drink inside her and I resented the fact that it took
alcohol to loosen her emotions. 'I don't know,' I would
reply, building up that wall all over again.

I knew that she was living with great loneliness. She
began to sleep on the sofa, just as I had done as a child.
It was as though the bed, and the flat itself, were now
too large for her.

One night she cried and I tried to comfort her, telling her things would get better, like a mother reassuring a child.

'It doesn't get better,' she said, looking at me despairingly. 'It gets worse.'

These days when I went home, I found myself
sitting in the way my father had, sprawled on the sofa
to watch the television, hands linked behind my head. I
ate from a plate on my lap and took off my shoes,
throwing them into the same corner where my dad had
thrown his. I was occupying the very space he had
occupied, literally trying to take his place. I knew so
very well how an absence could grow to be stronger
than a presence.

As I passed the milestone of my thirtieth birthday, I
remained single but my life was full. I had plenty of
friends, a lot of them gay men. I felt safe with them,
perhaps because, unlike my straight friends, they put no

pressure on me to 'settle down'. We were all perpetual adolescents, many of us in denial. With the spectre of AIDS beginning to cast its shadow, there was a growing, often unspoken, sense in the gay community that everyone might as well enjoy life while they could. Those hedonistic days of laughter and parties suited me right down to the ground as I was making up for lost time, as well as over-compensating for the long, depressing weekends in the East End. However, if I had a great social life, I had to manage it on very little money. Ten years after buying my Wimbledon flat, the mortgage remained a burden.

Mark was by this time living in Brussels, playing jazz guitar and running a music bar, but I now had another buddy – a guy called Seb, a student at the National Film School in Beaconsfield. I'd met him briefly ten years earlier, but he'd then moved to San Francisco for a while. When he came back to London we became good friends, and through him I'd developed an interest in film-making and writing scripts and plays. I acted in one of Seb's student films, playing the part of a girl who is hired to burst out of a cake at a fancy-dress party but is delivered, in the cake, to the wrong address.

Seb was living at 178b Westbourne Grove in Notting Hill which, before the advent of the yuppies, was a far cry from the fashionable area it is today. Its population was a mix of hippies, West Indians and bedsit-dwellers left over from the era of the notorious racketeering landlord Peter Rachman in the 1950s and 1960s. The

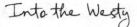

property – a three-storey house on the corner of
Ledbury Road, with a shop unit at the front on the
ground floor – belonged to Annie, an English hippy
who had long since disappeared to California. She never
asked for rent from anyone who lived there, only for the
house to be maintained and respected. Seb had taken it
over from a previous 'caretaker' on his return from the
States.

A year after graduating from film school, Seb
suggested I sold my flat and moved into his rent-free
pad in Notting Hill. It was ridiculous, he reasoned, for
me to be scrimping and saving to pay my mortgage in
Wimbledon when there was a room going begging in
the heart of London at 'the Westy', as it was known by
all who visited. I'd struggled to hang on to my investment in bricks and mortar as some kind of security for
the future, but what the hell – I was thirty years old,
tired of being constantly skint and his offer was just
too tempting. I took the plunge.

When I arrived at the Westy, there was already
another lodger in situ: our friend Adam, a handsome,
six-foot-four builder more than qualified to manage any
household repairs. However, after Adam married and
moved to the south of France, Seb's habit of knocking
down supporting walls was to cause a few problems. In
my room on the lower floor, a cavernous crack suddenly
opened up from floor to ceiling, to add to my existing
woes. A pair of elegant French windows near my bed
failed to close properly and someone had bodged the

job of creating a cat flap in one of the panels. In spite of all my attempts to block the opening, wintry mornings would often start with an Arctic wind blowing a small snowdrift on to my bedside rug. There was no central heating, just an archaic Ascot water-heater on the kitchen wall which spewed forth a scalding hot stream like an Italian coffee machine.

In a sense, the Westy was a much bigger version of the house in which I'd grown up. The difference was that Seb managed to fill it with wonderful things: a beautiful old bevelled mirror, a large 1950s American refrigerator, a pale-blue wartime gas cooker. When I'd arrived, the only way to get out on to the roof terrace was by climbing clumsily through the living-room window. Seb hired a friend to punch a hole through the wall and install a set of doors. Then he added a sound system and *voilà* – the scene was set for the Westy to become the best social venue in town.

The unit at the front of the building on the street level was occupied by an estate agency, and after their office closed for the day there was nobody to complain about loud music. Then the Westy would be transformed into a party house and informal 'knock and drop in centre', attracting a diverse mix of characters. The roof terrace was an ideal vantage point from which to view the Notting Hill carnival, so at August Bank Holiday weekends upwards of fifty people might stop by for the day, bearing bottles of wine and carnival whistles. Other days proved only slightly less busy.

After graduating from film school, Seb's ambition had been to direct drama but this was the 1980s, the age of MTV, and there was a big demand for people to direct pop promos, the hot new way to sell records. Soon he was making videos for Prince, Madness, Kirsty MacColl and a band called Five Star who, at the time, were the English Jackson Five. He also directed a rock series for Italian TV, presented by Ronnie Wood of the Stones.

Seb was not just a great director but a true 'social animal'. Funny and lovable, he made friends with everyone. The only trouble was, I was still trying to hold down my nine-to-five job. I'd come home from work to find members of Status Quo in the living room, or the dance troupe Hot Gossip. In the evenings, we'd go to concerts or parties, mixing with the likes of Kid Creole and his Coconuts. It was all slightly surreal, and I was finding it increasingly tough to get to work on time, especially when our landlady sent eccentric friends over from the States. They would sometimes arrive at a moment's notice to spend a few days or weeks in London partying or sightseeing, and several of them never managed to adjust to British time.

The most memorable of all our house guests was the Hollywood actress Elizabeth Ashley. Elizabeth was the ex-wife of George Peppard, whose finest hour had been co-starring with Audrey Hepburn in the 1961 classic movie *Breakfast at Tiffany's*. By the 1980s, however, he was better known – to younger audiences, at least – as the cigar-chomping leader of a renegade commando squad in the TV series *The A-Team*.

Why Elizabeth preferred to stay at the Westy rather than somewhere like the Dorchester hotel was anyone's guess. When we heard that she was coming Seb and I surmised that, as a friend of Annie, she must be a Boho rebel. If we were excited or amused at the prospect of having a star in our home, a visit from Barbara, her PA, soon brought us back down to earth. Barbara had a 'Hills' accent, an improbable bosom and an inexhaustible checklist. She was here to 'prepare the way' for her boss and to ensure that the facilities were fully up to standard. She turned up on a hot summer's day and top of her list was air-conditioning. Seb and I pointed to a dodgy window propped open by a single chopstick.

Outside the house, Barbara smiled a nervous goodbye and stepped hastily into a waiting cab. A few days later, Elizabeth Ashley appeared on our doorstep. In spite of all our shortcomings, she fitted into the Westy perfectly.

Elizabeth was in her early forties but had the low, rasping voice of an older woman. Her conversation was copious and peppered with Peppard, which was how she always referred to her ex-husband. The second of his five wives – he was still on number four at the time – she had met him on the set of *The Carpetbaggers* in the early 1960s, and though she went on to make several more movies, she said she always felt more at home on the stage. She had been fêted as a young theatre actress, earning Tony nominations for her Broadway performance as Corie in *Barefoot in the Park* and Maggie in *Cat on a Hot Tin Roof.* Her next role was to be Babette Van Degan in *The Two Mrs Grenvilles*, an American mini-series that would go on to win a number of Emmy Awards, one, bizarrely, for Outstanding Achievement in Hairstyling.

Having a Hollywood actress in the house served only to heighten the sense of unreality that already existed at the Westy. It became clear from her conversation that Elizabeth had plenty of professional integrity and no wish, as she put it, to become the kind of actress who fed lines such as 'Gee, how did you *do* that?' to the likes of Lee Majors. She also had no desire for anyone to stand on ceremony for her. Nevertheless, as I trotted off to work in the mornings I would pass Seb heading up the rickety stairs carrying a breakfast tray for our guest consisting of a boiled egg in a cracked cup. After a hard day at the office I would come home to sink at least a bottle of wine as I listened, fascinated but exhausted, to Elizabeth's tales.

She didn't exactly play the Hollywood game, which was why she preferred not to stay at swanky hotels. She told us about the sailboat she owned and how she used it as a refuge from the madness of the celebrity merry-go-round. In the mornings she would often appear in the kitchen looking frail and fragile, stick-thin in an old, oversized T-shirt. But then the doorbell would ring, signalling the arrival of extravagant bouquets from the likes of Rex Harrison. When she had an invitation to lunch, she would go upstairs to get ready and descend at the appointed hour looking every inch the star, an amazing outfit clinging to her clothes-horse body, completed by a wide-brimmed hat shielding a beautifully made-up face.

The summer days rolled by. Eventually Barbara appeared on our doorstep once more, this time to supervise the exodus of Elizabeth's luggage. Our house guest was returning to the States.

Seb and I waved goodbye as a car whisked Elizabeth off to the airport. It turned a corner and disappeared from view, leaving us standing on the pavement, just looking at each other.

'Did that really happen?' asked Seb.

We wondered for a moment whether perhaps we had dreamed the visit. It was like a story in a magazine. I was learning that life could be stranger than fiction.

Chapter Ten

A Clock Stops Ticking

On the eve of one hot August Bank Holiday weekend, I headed for Gullane House straight from a
meeting about the BBC's Children in Need appeal,
having volunteered to man the phones during the
forthcoming telethon. My own child, Sarah Louise, was
now fourteen years old and, I sincerely hoped, in need
of nothing. In four years' time she would have the right
to acquire her original birth certificate. Would she try
to find me?

I was baffled to find my mother's maisonette empty.
As I put the kettle on, wondering where she could
have got to, the telephone rang. An aunt in Kent
with whom we were rarely in contact was on the other
end of the line, telling me that my mum had been taken
ill.

At St Thomas' Hospital in Westminster, I found her
perched on the edge of a bed, wearing a strange

nightgown. When she turned to look at me I saw fear in her eyes.

A doctor explained that she'd had some kind of fit at work the day before. The only telephone number in her bag was my aunt's, which was why the hospital hadn't been able to notify me. My mother was confused and disorientated. Unsure of what to do, I called her older sister Bett, who arrived from Becontree with my cousin Danny. We hadn't seen one another for years but I was grateful to have family to lean on in this crisis.

The doctors gave my mum an MRI scan and eventually decided that the fit might have been an isolated incident. She was discharged into my care and sent home with drugs usually prescribed for epilepsy to prevent further fits.

My mother never recovered. Within three months she had developed a kind of dementia. Her body became weak on one side and she took terrifying tumbles down the stairs but she refused point blank to go back to the hospital. She wouldn't even see the doctor.

One night I dissolved into tears of frustration. 'It's just one of those things,' she said. Then she shuffled into the kitchen and returned with a cup of tea for me. I knew how much effort it had taken her to do this and I watched her set down the cup with a trembling hand. We had never talked properly to each other, but this simple gesture expressed more than words ever could.

Night after night I watched her staring up at the clock on the wall. Whatever time it showed, she would make the same remark. 'Is that all it is?'

Finally, the clock stopped ticking.

I managed to get my mother admitted to hospital, where doctors belatedly diagnosed an aggressive lesion to the brain. My bosses at work were sympathetic and I was given compassionate leave, which meant I was able to visit her every day. Due to the dementia, she became childlike in the last months of her life. I would feed her from a spoon and try to interest her in the magazines she had always loved to read. But when I gave them to her, after looking at the pictures she would put them to her mouth and chew them like a teething baby.

One day, sitting down at her bedside, I noticed that her watch was missing. I searched her cabinet but couldn't find it anywhere. She had no need to know what time it was, or that it was running out for her, but I felt the loss on her behalf. The watch had been given to her by Kardomah and on the back were engraved the words: 'In gratitude for twenty-five years' faithful service'. I had no option but to take off the rings she was still wearing on her fingers. She protested but I couldn't stand the thought that these, too, might be stolen from her in the night.

My mum always wore her wedding ring and another single gold band that had belonged to her mother, Julia Shea, the Irish grandmother I had never known as she had died when I was just a month old. I put the rings on to my own fingers for safekeeping and there they would remain for many years.

My mother finally faded away in December 1984 and after her funeral, friends rallied round to help me clear out the flat. I gave away all but one volume of *The Book of Knowledge*, but kept the photographs my mum and I had pasted into albums: snapshots of me as a baby, crawling across a lawn in Kew Gardens as my father laughs behind me. Two pages later, I'm standing by a tree, again at Kew, in a knitted hat, double-breasted coat and reins. Then come summers spent at Pontin's holiday camps, my mother in her long sleeves in the sun. I found certificates for weddings, births and funerals; a black-edged card commemorating my Uncle Johnny's cremation. And a council rent book.

Someone commented that I should keep on the flat – council flats were like gold dust in those days – but I knew it was time to move on. I had spent ten years trying to live my mother's life for her; now I wanted to live my own.

At first I felt a sense of relief that my mum had been released from her suffering but that was soon replaced by a sudden, piercing grief. For months I'd been worrying about her health, fearing that I might have to move back into Gullane House – perhaps for years. As I hadn't known what was wrong with her until so late in the day I'd had no idea how long she might go on living, deteriorating all the while, in that terrible twilight. Having sustained her for so long with the events of my life, now, every time I had some snippet of news to tell her, I would automatically reach for the phone before remembering that she wasn't there any more. I thought of all the conversations we'd never had, and never would have, and wished we'd been more open with each other, about everything, before it was too late.

One positive to come out of my loss was that I had grown closer to Aunt Bett, who had been a great help since my mother had first fallen ill and had stoically made the journey into Westminster on the District Line from Becontree to visit her regularly when she had gone back into hospital. I kept loosely in touch with Bett for the rest of her life, ringing her from time to time, sending her postcards from abroad and making sure I remembered her birthday.

Aunt Bett wasn't able to shed much light on the enigma that was my mother but she did supply a few additional details. She confirmed what my mum had told me about her marriage to George Townsend, and the big house with the piano. George and my young mother had been besotted with each other, according to Bett: 'If you ever went round to visit them she'd be sitting on his lap, gazing into his eyes.' George, I learned, had been broken-hearted when my mother had left him and had apparently suffered some kind of nervous breakdown. Nobody was sure whether he had ever really recovered.

After my conversation with my mother about George I had understood how the memory of the more gracious surroundings that had once been hers must have tortured her in the nineteen long years of coping with Lefevre Road. Having talked to Aunt Bett, I also began to reflect on what a huge event this early marital break-up must have been for my mother. Not only had divorce been rare in working-class marriages then, but her family were, for the most part, incredibly strict Catholics. Apart from my mum and Uncle Johnny. No wonder they had been close. Johnny must have been disillusioned by his terrible wartime experiences and my mother, in all probability, by being branded – or at least perceiving herself to be – a scarlet woman. They both drank and smoked all their lives to help them deal with the stress. I heard her voice echoing down the years. 'There'll be no place in heaven for me,' she would joke with my father. 'I'll be damned for marrying you.' Perhaps a part of her had actually believed that.

The odd piece of the puzzle was slotting into place. I saw why my mother had been so much older than all the other mini-skirted East End mums of my childhood: she had a history. She had been walking another path before our family had even existed. Like me, she had reached a fork in the road and chosen the path less travelled. But what she felt about that, and the inner life she led, had always been a mystery to me and would now remain so forever.

The realisation that I was a thirty-two-year-old orphan came as something of a jolt. My closest blood relative was Sarah Louise, who was even more of a mystery to me than my mother. When I went back to do a last sweep of the maisonette at Gullane House before surrendering the keys to the council, I found a tiny plastic wristband at the back of a drawer in my bedroom where it had lain for fourteen years.

The letters have faded but I know what they spell. Sarah Louise is out there somewhere – a teenager now, almost a young woman. What does she look like? Is she straightening her hair? Does she clash with her teachers as I once did? Can she talk to her mother in a way I never could to mine? Perhaps she doesn't even know the circumstances of her birth. But I cling to the belief that one day she will read my name on a certificate and we will see each other again.

I take a last look around me and make a decision. I put the bracelet back into the drawer and close it. I need no reminders of Sarah Louise. She lives in my heart and I take her with me wherever I go. I walk out of my teenage bedroom – the room where she grew inside me – down the stairs and out on to the balcony, locking the front door behind me.

Having been tied to my mother for so long, now that the cord had been cut I felt as if I were in freefall. I acknowledged that I needed to look for positives in my loss and see this release as a liberation. When a friend mentioned to me in passing that a man she knew was looking for crew for his yacht and asked me if I fancied going sailing, I saw only a new opportunity. Why not? Since my father's death I had spent no more than a few weeks out of the country – seven days in Ibiza, a fortnight in Greece, a few holidays in Spain – but now I was free to do whatever I liked and to go wherever I liked.

I took the number I was offered for 'the Captain' and plucked up the courage to dial it. When I could make out what he was saying – he had an almost impenetrable Glasgow accent – I discovered that he was in fact a friend of a friend. We agreed to meet when he was next in London.

Knowing nothing whatsoever about sailing, I turned to the Dewey classification system and set out purposefully for my local library. There I found a book packed with aerial views of a bullet-shaped vessel attempting manoeuvres in what looked like a choppy sea. A section headed 'Beating' explained how a yacht could sail into an opposing wind. It was perhaps no coincidence that the next chapter was entitled 'Man Overboard'.

A few weeks later I walked into the Portobello Gold pub and immediately spotted the Captain standing at the bar. He wasn't hard to identify since he was wearing a reefer jacket thick enough to weather a hurricane. As he turned, I saw that his face was half-hidden by a nautical beard. He was somewhere in his late forties, very rugged, with fiery red hair, though a little grey was creeping into his whiskers. His eyes were a startling sea blue.

'You must be Julie,' he smiled. As he ordered me a glass of wine, I watched him knock back a large Glenmorangie as though it were a glass of water. Pulling over a bar stool, he invited me to take a seat and I clambered on to it, a little clumsily owing to my high heels. He was looking down at them with an expression that suggested he had never before seen a pair of women's shoes.

'What the hell are those?'

I stretched out a foot to show off a pair of brand-new black stilettos with dainty ankle straps. I'd bought them in Shepherd's Bush market but they had the look of something far more expensive. I always wore high heels, even when cycling to work, which I did most days. The bike ruined the shanks on a lot of them. But I just couldn't reconcile myself to being five-foot-four and a precious half-an-inch. I felt like a tall person in a short person's body.

'Nice, aren't they?'

The Captain turned up his nose as if I had a couple of stale halibut on my feet. 'Get shot of 'em,' he commanded. 'And buy yourself a pair of these, or you'll be over the side at the first tack.' He raised his own foot. I raised my eyebrows. I hadn't worn wellington boots since primary school.

The Captain asked how old I was.

This did not seem to me altogether polite, but I took it in my stride. 'Thirty-two.'

'Thirty-two and you've never set foot on a sail boat before?'

I explained that I'd never had the chance before. He fixed me with a steely look and inquired about my health. I told him it was fine and inquired about his.

'Oh, I'm fit and healthy,' he said. 'But then, I lead a different life from you London people, cooped up in offices and drinking clubs.'

He downed another Scotch. Thus fortified, he seemed slightly more subdued. He sighed, blue eyes narrowing as if he were staring off at some far horizon. When he spoke his voice was quieter. 'There's a beautiful world out there for those who want to see it. And the best way to do that is from a boat.'

I asked him about the places he'd been and he began to count off countries on calloused fingers. Having covered most of Europe, he started on the Far East.

'... Thailand, Singapore, Malaysia, Indonesia. My old father was a bandsman in the British Army, played the trumpet in Burma. He's spent the rest of his life in Ayrshire but he's never settled to civvy life. Still tells me all his stories, paints pictures of the places he went to. The one he missed out on was somewhere called Sulawesi. Ever heard of it?'

I shook my head. Geography had never been my strong point.

'Well, we made a bargain. I'd make the visit for him. Proxy, you might say.'

The Captain threw another whisky down his throat and bought me another drink. Slowly, circuitously, his story emerged. I gathered that as a young man he had spent several freezing seasons fishing the Arctic waters of the Barents Sea before building up a business buying fishing boats in Norway, selling them in Scotland and sailing them down there. Britain's entry into the EEC had somehow affected the economics of this enterprise so he had shut up shop and ploughed some of his profits into making the trip to Bulukumba in south-west Sulawesi – not just for his father's sake, but because he, too, harboured a dream: of owning a vessel called a phinisi, an Indonesian copy of an eighteenth-century sailing boat.

The Captain cleared his throat. 'It was a romantic notion,' he admitted. 'The boats are crude, to put it mildly, and the government makes it hard to get them out of the country unless big money changes hands. So I got myself a job in Singapore. I'm a Rolls-Royce engineer by trade and managed to find a good position with an oil company while it was possible for foreigners to make a living on the oil patch. After a while I did get myself a boat – not a phinisi, but a yacht that was good enough to sail away in.'

All the while the Captain was talking, he was making sketches on a series of beer mats. When he had finished, he handed me two diagrams of boats. The first, a phinisi, did indeed look like 'a romantic notion' – a majestic galleon, keeled over under full sail – while the other seemed a smaller, more conventional vessel.

He introduced her as the *Hei Lung*. 'That's the one I bought in Singapore,' he explained. 'The name means Water Dragon. Or at least, I think it does.'

Knowing nothing at all about boat design, I made appreciative noises. The Captain, however, was still dreamily considering the boat's lines, as though he was admiring the curves on a beautiful woman. He spoke about her in the same way. 'A crazy American fell in love with her just as I was running low on money. When I told him I wasn't interested, he kept offering more and more. In the end, he simply made me an offer I couldn't refuse.'

His hand wandered to another beer mat and the sketching began again. He hadn't yet asked me a thing about my credentials as possible crew. Instead he just kept passing me beer mats, like a man far from home sharing family snapshots.

'This boat's by the same designer as the one I have now but you can see the difference: the Vertue's a classic design but she's only eight metres with one mast.

'That's a sloop,' he went on, 'whereas the boat I have now is a ketch – two masts with mizzens stepped forward of the rudder post.'

I greeted the explanation of each new nautical feature with a businesslike nod of approval. He had ordered me a new glass of wine for every Glenmorangie he had swallowed, so maybe it was the alcohol but, even though I didn't have a clue what he was talking about, I was becoming increasingly enamoured of the idea of a life on the ocean wave. Especially after his tales of peeing on a whale and sailing the Malacca Straits more than a dozen times without ever seeing a single pirate.

As the bell rang for closing time, the Captain picked up his loose change from the bar, drained his final glass of whisky and glanced at a huge submariner's watch.

'The boat's on the Isle of Wight. *Golden Sunset*. Easy enough to find. Come down in a week's time. It'll be a shakedown cruise to Norway first to see my kids and my ex-wife.'

'Right. And, er ... can you tell me how long you expect we'll be away?'

The Captain shrugged. 'If the weather's fine, a couple of weeks, but if we've got storms to wait out, make it three. Hell, give it a month. You never know, you might just want to stay on for another trip.'

By now, more than a little tipsy, I was swaying. I felt my foot slipping out of its stiletto heel.

'Where to?'

The Captain smiled. 'Somewhere warm, dry—' the barman suddenly broke in, bellowing something about whether or not we had homes to go to '—and away from English licensing laws.'

The Captain smiled and held out his hand to me. It was like shaking a friendly loofah. 'I'm looking forward to sailing with you, Julie. I think we're going to get along fine.' For maybe the first time all evening, his voice was mellow. 'See you next week.'

My vision slightly blurred, I followed his progress to the door. He paused for a moment and looked back at my shoes. 'And make sure you leave the deck-staplers behind.' With that he was gone.

As I weaved my own way home, stepping out of the way of a handful of drunks brawling on the Portobello Road, rain had begun to fall, but it didn't bother me unduly. With a head full of dreams and a pocketful of beer mats, a week seemed a long time to wait.

Chapter Eleven

Tramontana

I soon discovered that the Captain was always on the look-out for people to go sailing with him. Although one or two mutual acquaintances had crewed for him, nobody seemed to enjoy it much, for some reason. But it was too late for anyone to talk me out of it: I was already hooked on the idea. The Captain was clearly one of life's eccentrics, but I'd also found him strangely engaging. All the same, I had the sense not to go alone. On the phone he had agreed to another 'shipmate' coming with me on the voyage and I knew just the right person to take along.

I'd originally met Maggie at work. A couple of years older than I was, she had been to drama school and oozed confidence. Between acting roles, she was an occasional secretary and sometimes demonstrated such items as miracle ironing-board covers at posh department stores, where she always managed to sell more than anybody else because she threw herself whole-heartedly into the task at hand. She was also smart, practical and game for a laugh. I couldn't think of a better companion to have at sea.

A week after my first meeting with the Captain, having taken practically all my holiday leave, I travelled down with Maggie to Cowes one evening. By the time we found the marina it was dark and the weather was atrocious. We walked up and down quay after quay, in driving rain, searching for the boat until Maggie finally shrieked above the wind: 'Over here!'

I hurried across to where she was standing, waving at me. I could just about make out the words *Golden Sunset* on the stern of the boat Maggie had pointed out. On her mooring, the fifty-foot ketch looked bigger than I had imagined. We knocked gently on the hull, then clambered aboard with our sopping-wet parachute bags. We waited, full of trepidation. A few moments later, a door swung open to reveal the Captain, wearing nothing but a sarong.

'Welcome!' he boomed, and quickly turned to go back inside. Maggie shot me a worried glance. I hoped this wasn't a sign of things to come. Down in the *Golden Sunset*'s broad saloon, the Captain explained that his inappropriate attire was due to him having been in the shower. Handing us each a glass of beer, he stepped into his cabin to get dressed. 'Sorry about the weather.'

Outside the wind howled and halyards clanked like cowbells as the tethered boat bucked the waves. 'No

problem,' I called back. 'Maggie and I are good swim-
mers.' We exchanged a smile but the Captain suddenly
re-emerged, in jeans and a nautical sweater, looking
unamused. 'That won't help much in a force 9 gale.'

He picked up his beer from the saloon table and took
a deep swig. Maggie and I charged our own glasses,
smiles slipping.

That night we made ourselves as comfortable as we
could in a tiny cabin dominated by damp bunk beds. I
took the top one, with a view out of a small, leaky scut-
tle. All I could see outside was driving rain and masts
ducking and weaving in the wind. A gruff voice sounded
suddenly outside our door. 'Ready for lights out, ladies?'

'Sure,' I replied breezily.

'Sweet dreams.'

A switch was thrown and the Captain headed off
towards his cabin. In the darkness, I heard Maggie
whisper urgently: 'What have you got us into?'

We were laid up in Cowes, waiting for the weather to
break, for several days. In the meantime, Maggie and I
were given a few basic instructions. The conditions
only ever improved marginally but the Captain, bored
and frustrated, made an impatient decision to set sail in
a force 8 wind. Maggie looked this up on the Beaufort
scale in my library book. '"Fresh gale,"' she read out
loud, '"winds thirty-nine to forty-six miles per hour.
Moderately high waves with breaking crests forming
spindrift." Whatever that is.' She gave a small shrug
and continued.

'"Well-marked streaks of foam blowing along wind direction and considerable airborne spray."' We looked at one another.

'Isn't there anything that makes more sense?'

Maggie flicked over the page. 'There's this.' She began reading a description better geared to land-dwellers. '"Twigs broken from trees. Cars veer on the road. Progress on foot seriously impeded."' She closed the book and glared at me somewhat accusingly.

I reminded myself that I was supposed to be looking for positives among the negatives. I searched desperately for one. 'He must know what he's doing, Mags.'

'Really?' She seemed decidedly unimpressed.

All we could do was hope for the best.

The Captain had managed to recruit a local man to take care of the engine room. Al was just coming out of it when we first met, a short, stocky man with a dark, weatherbeaten face, gypsy-black eyelashes framing his pale-grey eyes. As he smiled, I couldn't fail to notice that every other tooth in his grin was missing.

'You must be ADH Julie.'

He saw my confusion.

'Able Deck Hand,' he supplied. 'That's what you'll be from now on.'

'I don't known about "able",' I ventured. 'I'm new to all this.'

'You'll be fine,' said Al reassuringly. 'Sailing's just a matter of common sense.'

With that he disappeared back down into the hellhole of an engine room. I crouched down to see what was going on in there. Bilge water slopped around his ankles and I could make out noisy engine pistons rising and falling in the cramped space. The air was fast becoming thick with the smell of diesel until Al closed the door. From the other side, I could have sworn I heard the snap and fizz of a ring pull being removed from a can of beer.

Maggie had gone off with the Captain in a dinghy to buy provisions and returned looking anxious. 'You didn't tell him I was vegetarian,' she hissed. 'He's just gone and bought a year's supply of cold cuts.'

I tried to keep up her spirits. 'Don't worry. I'll make sure you don't get scurvy.'

I could tell from Maggie's expression that she hadn't recovered her sense of humour.

We spent the rest of the afternoon battening hatches and stowing breakables. In stark contrast to the filthy engine room, the rest of the boat was comfortable and stylish with all mod cons. It was kitted out in teak with white leather upholstery and boasted 13 amp power run off a generator so I could even plug in my heated hair rollers. I didn't dare own up to the Captain that I had brought them along but everyone was to find out when they caused our navigation lights to fail just as we were trying to dodge a bunch of ferries and cruisers in the Channel.

It wasn't an easy voyage. We were beating into head-winds, tacking northwards with the boat on her ear most of the way. 'By the time we reach Norway you'll think you've one leg shorter than the other!' the Captain laughed over the wind, like a demented Ahab. 'Haul in!' he shouted at us. 'Trim sails!' Or, while he hauled in or trimmed the sails, 'Take the wheel!' The rain lashed down but somehow I always managed to find time for a slick of lipstick, which I felt I needed even when wearing a survival suit.

On the second day out, we lost a vital piece of chart after Maggie stood a wet coffee mug on it. 'Don't tell him it was me!' she implored. The Captain reckoned he could plot an alternative course if only somebody could remember Pythagoras's theorem. It fell to me to recall a verse from a childhood spent absorbing radio music almost by osmosis: a cheerful number sung by Danny Kaye about the square of the hypotenuse of a right triangle being equal to the sum of the square of the two adjacent sides.

The Captain wasn't a fan of Danny Kaye but the song saved the day and he admitted that he would rather sail with learners who were good company than a 'boy racer who's willing to risk my boat for a few thrills'.

Mindful of Maggie's dietary requirements, I made vegetarian spaghetti, which slipped straight off plates on to already damp sweaters. Some way off the Danish coast, we ran out of water. The Captain didn't seem too concerned as he had plenty of alcoholic supplies on board. 'And what do we brush our teeth in?' asked

Maggie. The Captain tossed her a can of lager. If Maggie was exasperated, Al seemed to find beer a useful all-purpose substitute. Now, whenever the engine-room door opened, I could see plenty of empty cans floating on top of the bilge water.

In spite of all this, somehow I managed to enjoy the voyage, appreciating what I now knew to be the object of the exercise: putting oneself though a lot of hardship in order to earn some enjoyable respite in a far-flung port. Our first port, however, turned out to be not so far-flung. Still in a howling gale, we limped into Esberg in Denmark to take on water. There was only one problem: dehydrated and somewhat confused, we had forgotten to take down the little mizzen sail with the result that, no matter how hard we tried to steer towards port, we kept being blown away from the quay by an offshore wind. Dry land was so tantalisingly close, and yet we just couldn't reach it.

When at long last we docked, Maggie was first out on to the quay and so pleased to be back on terra firma that she kissed the ground and promptly went straight off to find a ferry to take her home. I couldn't blame her, but her premature departure meant she missed the best part of the trip. The next morning I awoke to an unfamiliar and initially unnerving silence: the wind was no longer screaming through the rigging. I went on deck to see a miracle unfolding: we were gliding through the smooth, mirror-like waters of a Norwegian fjord.

The Captain spent a week with his children for Sommerfest, with Al and me as background crew. In this more relaxed environment, I began properly to learn the ropes – or rather lines, sheets and warps, as they're more usually referred to on a boat. I swabbed decks, set sail and kept things generally shipshape. On midsummer night the Captain's teenage children joined us and we decorated the boat with flower garlands. The Captain gave me a handful of Norwegian kroner and encouraged me to placate the sea gods by throwing the coins overboard. We drank aquavit and watched fireworks filling the sky with coloured light, reflected in the shimmering fjord below. Night barely fell at all over the water. It was magical.

I was far from London and everything I knew, but somehow I felt at home in this sea gypsy's life. I knew we would soon be returning and when the Captain came to find me on deck one morning, I assumed it was to tell me we'd be setting off that day. Instead he said: 'How do you fancy coming along on another trip?'

This wasn't what I had been expecting. He could see that in my eyes. He could also see that I was tempted. 'Hell, just do it! You've no ties in London, have you?'

I thought for a moment. If I didn't do something like this now, when I was completely free for the first time in my life and the opportunity was there for the taking, when would I do it? The money I still had from selling my flat would allow me to give up work for a while. I would be able to do more writing than I was managing at the Westy, and the Captain was right: I had lots of people in my life, good friends, but no ties, now, other than those I kept in my heart. As I looked out over a Norwegian fjord, I remembered a song from long ago – the one I had sung with my cousins outside a riverside pub at the Wapping docks.

> … *Though the night be dark as dungeon*
> *Not a star to be seen above*
> *I will be guided without stumble*
> *Into the arms of my only love.*

I told the Captain another trip sounded like a good idea.

I returned to London, handed in my notice at work and ended up spending the best part of four years sailing with the Captain. Seb was happy to keep my room at the Westy for me and I would go home from time to time for a week or so, usually when the boat was in dry dock or the winter weather too foul to sail in, to see my friends, visit Mark's parents – to whom I'd grown very close – in Tunbridge Wells and generally catch up with London life.

After the Norway trip, we sailed to Ireland, taking the *Golden Sunset* from Inverness to Fort William down through the Caledonian Canal and the Highland lochs, joined for part of the time by the Captain's teenage daughter. The Captain was restless and keen to test the boat with a long voyage. He wanted to sail the Atlantic and investigate chartering possibilities in the

Caribbean, which meant getting to Portugal by the autumn, the optimum time to make the crossing. I was up for it. My London friends thought I was mad. A couple of weeks sailing to Norway was one thing, but this was, they suggested, a little extreme. Some of them suspected I was running away from the real world, and perhaps I was. 'Are you sure you don't want to join the circus instead?' asked my friend Theresa, rather drily.

The problem was that the Captain didn't know the Caribbean very well – his territory was the Far East – and his plans were vague. He dithered about where we should go, the French islands or the British ones, and I capitalised on his indecision by encouraging him to make a detour via the Mediterranean. I was dying to cruise the Med, envisaging a sort of nautical Grand Tour taking in places I had read about in the works of Gerald Durrell and Henry James – the Greek islands, Naples, Capri, Sardinia... So we sailed to northern Spain, then all the way down the coast of Portugal, leaving the boat in a swish marina for a while to have it painted up. After that we set off for southern Spain.

By the time we reached Portugal we had fallen for each other. The Captain was not by any means my usual type. I had always gone for artistic-looking men, tall, slender and long-haired, almost androgynous. Yet as I got to know my sailing companion I found myself increasingly attracted to him. He was a real tough guy, but he was also a terrific character, very intelligent and had a good heart.

In retrospect I wonder whether after my mother died I was somehow giving myself permission to seek out a man more like my father, someone big and strong who would look after me. It's not uncommon for a mother to be a little jealous of the father–daughter relationship, and it occurs to me that, in our family triangle, this might have been the case with my mum. As a couple they'd had a great life before I was born, when she'd travelled around with my father to his darts tournaments, drinking, socialising and having fun. Then, all of a sudden, I'd arrived, all that had stopped, and some of the love, pride and attention previously reserved for her had been focused on me. Perhaps, to avoid encroaching on her territory, I'd learned to reject men cast in my father's mould but now that she was gone maybe I was looking for my dad again. Or maybe it was just that, having lost both of them, I was simply searching for somebody to fill a protective role. Whatever the reason, the Captain and I formed a double-act of sorts: two misfits sharing a love of travel and adventure.

From southern Spain we cruised the Balearics – docking at Mallorca, Ibiza and Menorca. On several occasions the *Golden Sunset* ended up stuck on Menorca for a considerable length of time because… well, mainly because it was a fabulous island. One of these spells, however, was prompted by a genuine emergency.

In the Balearics, we received word that the Captain's mother had died. He had to get back to Scotland as a matter of urgency for the funeral, to look after his old dad, who was in his eighties, and to sort out his father's domestic arrangements afterwards. That meant leaving me with a fifty-foot ketch I wasn't capable of handling on my own. We had to find somewhere to moor it, and me, for the duration.

A friend of mine had spent a holiday in somebody's villa in the Menorcan countryside near the port of Ciudadella, the old capital, a lovely medieval town. It would be ideal, Richard told me on the phone. It had a beautiful harbour, and lots of wonderful little restaurants, and he was sure if I went there and found this 'guy called Manolo' he would help me with the boat. So we set sail for Ciudadella, in the west of Menorca, and it did indeed prove to be an enchanting town. We dropped anchor and I waved the Captain off to Scotland.

We could have gone to Menorca's main port, Mahón, on the opposite side of the island in the south-east: an eight-mile-long sleeve of a harbour known as one of the safest in the Med. Instead I found myself in one of the most dangerous. I didn't know that Ciudadella was prone to a phenomenon known locally as the *rissaga* – a meteorological tsunami, which is like a flood tide, but created by atmospheric pressure rather than anything tidal. Soon after I arrived there I went ashore to have dinner in one of the harbourside restaurants. When I got back to the boat I was horrorstruck to discover that it seemed to have sunk: it was sitting so low in the water. On the quay, the fishermen were calling to me, 'Capitana Julie! Capitana Julie! You must get your boat out now!'

'*No puedo!*' I shrieked. Then, giving up on my school-girl Spanish, 'I can't! I don't know how!'

I could put up sails but there was no way I could manoeuvre the *Golden Sunset* in a small space like a harbour. Dressed for the evening in my high heels, I couldn't even manage to untie the mooring lines on my own, so I was in a nautical quandary. The fishermen had to steer the boat out of the harbour for me and anchor me up safely.

It turned out that this dramatic drop in the water level was one of the warning signs of a *rissaga*, which was why it was imperative that all the boats were moved. The fishermen were usually the first to notice any problem when they went down to the harbour at night, and they would quickly send the word round. Although there never actually was a *rissaga* while I was alone on the boat, the waterline fell dangerously low on several occasions. When it first happened I was panic-stricken. I'd envisaged nothing more than being parked in Ciudadella for a few weeks, sunning myself and enjoying a few cocktails on the poop deck, while I waited for the Captain to fly back from Scotland. I hadn't expected to have to actually *drive* the thing.

I racked my brains for some useful information but all I could summon was a dim memory of an old *Navy Lark* episode in which Leslie Phillips had offered the instruction, 'Left hand down a bit.' I was on the phone to the Captain every five minutes from the bar, pleading, 'You *have* to come back – the boat's in serious danger.' I was terrified that something would go horribly wrong. The last time there had been a *rissaga*, I had learned, all the water had receded from the port and a twenty-metre mini-tsunami had powered in, sweeping away cars on the shore road and destroying the harbourside restaurants.

But having to manage on my own meant I had to live on my wits and make friends not only with the fishermen, but also with the man who ran the tourist boat and other locals. Soon it became a matter of routine that, when the *rissaga* threatened, they would come aboard, steer the *Golden Sunset* to safety and bring me back again when the danger had passed. After a week or so my reputation spread and everyone in the port knew the Englishwoman who couldn't move her boat.

Reyes and Tanito, a young local couple who ran a bar, took me under their wing. I met people from other boats and before long I was caught up in the midsummer *fiesta*, San Joan, the biggest in the Menorcan calendar, which was marked by all sorts of traditional activities. I soon found it was one big, non-stop, three- or four-day party, fuelled by *pomada*, a poky cocktail of Mahón gin and lemonade, during which horses and riders took to the streets en masse, high-stepping through the crowd and even into people's houses. There was traditional music, jousting on the sands, men going

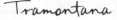

round with sheep on their backs and a strange custom involving people throwing sacks of hazelnuts at one another – a gesture of love, apparently.

When the Captain returned I was ashore and spotted his red head as he beetled his way along the quay, nervously scanning the harbour for the *Golden Sunset.* Once he saw that she was still in one piece he visibly relaxed. He had left behind a helpless ninny and returned to find a woman wearing a skipper's hat who knew almost everyone in Ciudadella. My Spanish had come on in leaps and bounds, too. It was all a bit disconcerting for the Captain but he took it well. For me, the realisation that I had coped on my own, albeit with a little help from my friends, was a turning point. It was a massive boost to my confidence.

Ciudadella became my home from home while we were at sea and we returned there often. I invited a couple of girlfriends there once, for a summer holiday, while the Captain was off somewhere. They were London ladies, party girls like me, and turned up on the quay with cases full of make-up and beauty products, high heels and heated rollers. The man who operated the tourist boat, whom I'd befriended during the *rissaga* crisis, was always infuriated by anyone tying their boat to his when the quay was too crowded for them to find a proper mooring. He had been known to untie the offending vessels in the middle of the night, setting them adrift. But he was so amused by the camp ladies of the *Golden Sunset* that he not only happily allowed us to tie up to his craft but also let us leave our stilettos on it when we teetered back after a night out ashore.

One morning we awoke on the *Golden Sunset,* somewhat hung over, to find ourselves in motion. Not only was my head thumping but my stomach was lurching too. As I came to, I realised that the tourist boat captain was at the wheel. A huge oil tanker had arrived and there hadn't been enough room for it to get into the harbour, so he'd simply jumped aboard and moved the boat for us without us even being aware of it.

'*Gracias!*' I called from my quarters.

'*De nada!*' he replied as he skipped off back to his pleasure boat.

The Captain and I kept ourselves afloat financially in the Med by chartering the boat for one-, two- or three-day trips. There were lots of beautiful places, including stunning, unspoiled beaches, within easy reach. Our service was, however, a little erratic. We once entertained a wedding party for a whole week: a wealthy couple from Milan, along with two of their friends, who had decided to do something a little different for their honeymoon. They found themselves having to sleep in bunk beds because the Captain refused to relinquish his cabin. They also did all the cooking, as they didn't consider mine to be up to Italian standards, and we had wonderful pasta every day. Strangely, they seemed to enjoy their cruise.

Not everyone did. We once took a family of Spanish holidaymakers out for a day, telling them they didn't really need to wear their lifejackets on this trip. The Captain, after one too many beers, grazed the hull on some rocks – which did make rather an alarming noise – and the kids began to cry while the parents rapidly made a beeline for the jackets. We returned to the harbour where, having had a couple of drinks myself by this time, I took the mooring lines, leaped from the bows and managed to miss the quay, slipping down the gap and disappearing from view. Our daytrippers literally ran off the boat screaming, the children barrelling down the quay as fast as their little legs would carry them, scarcely pausing to tear off the bright orange lifejackets and fling them back at us. The parents were right behind them, throwing us the money for the charter fee as they made a desperate escape.

I realised that making these short excursions around the Med for a day or so at a time and hanging around in port in between was not good for the Captain. It was clear he had a weakness for alcohol – though I can't pretend that came as much of a surprise to me after the number of Glenmorangies I'd seen him put away the evening we'd first met – and this way of life exacerbated matters. A long sea voyage was the one thing that always sorted him out. 'I've got to screw the nut' was his way of telling me he needed to go to sea for a while and dry out.

I was gregarious and loved meeting new people and socialising in the local bars where, by now, I could chat away in Spanish. Although the Captain was fluent in

Norwegian he struggled to learn any Spanish, so he preferred the ex-pat bars, where he would find new audiences for his tales of the Changi Sailing Club, which I'd heard over and over again. He was game enough, but at heart he was a loner, if a sociable one. I was perfectly content with my own company but for me a big part of the appeal of being at sea was the excitement of coming into port at a new, exotic place or returning to a favourite destination. The Captain was only ever really happy under sail.

Each morning was starting to feel like the dawn of another boring day in paradise. I'd always thought being aboard the boat would be a chance to do more writing but what with the daily chores, maintenance and all the partying ashore, there never seemed to be the time. I told the Captain I was ready for something different and suggested that maybe we really should be thinking now about the big voyage that he had always planned. Either that, or we could stay in the Med and charter the boat on a more businesslike footing – advertising with the proper chandlery companies, going to sea for longer, two weeks at a time, maybe getting a licence so we could do charter work in Italy, where they were more up on all the regulations. I reminded him that he was steadily going through his funds and they weren't being replenished. The Captain was hopeless with money and put everything he had into the boat. I was worried that if it were to need some enormous repair or, worse, sink, he would be stuffed.

Someone offered us a charter that would have given his finances a big boost. All we were asked to do to secure the job was smarten up the boat, as it looked a bit neglected. While we were in Mallorca I got the Captain to buy a job lot of deck paint and then I set to work. After painting the decks, I started on the carriage roof and completed it all while the Captain sat in the bar for two days. I was stiff from head to foot and my back was black from the sun. But then I noticed that the paint was blistering. What was going on? Slowly it dawned on me that whatever it was he had bought, it was certainly not pukka deck paint. I was so exasperated I just threw down my brush, jumped into the water and swam some distance to a beach. I went to stay with some friends ashore and didn't come back for several days.

When I did return we made up and anchored in an idyllic bay. I happened to wake early and was sure I could hear running water. I got up and investigated. Opening the door to the engine room, I found water well above the level of the duckboards. The Captain had forgotten to screw up the valve in the loo and sea water was coming into the boat. If it had gone on any longer we would have sunk.

I had always been a little in awe of the Captain's fearlessness and sailing prowess but a few silly mistakes like these made me wonder whether he was beginning to lose the plot, and this started to chip away at the great respect I had for him. I knew he liked the idea of being able to up anchor and leave everything behind him. But it meant that whenever he blotted his copy-book – made some kind of error, or had too much to drink somewhere – he could simply sail away, and as a result he never learned from his mistakes. He just went somewhere else and repeated them. While I was a Londoner and still had a home and friends in the capital, he was a wandering Scotsman who had never belonged in any big city. I realised that he really was the Flying Dutchman, doomed to sail the oceans forever.

At sea in the Balearics we encountered sudden bad weather. Trying to run from it, we headed straight into another weather system bringing with it high winds, gigantic waves and astonishing sheet lightning. We had to stick it out: there was nowhere else to run. The sails were down and we were at the mercy of the elements.

The northerly wind known as the tramontana was howling its way across the mountains of the islands. A relative of the French mistral, the tramontana can blow for over a week and is said to influence the psyche. There are stories of how it has driven people and animals alike to commit suicide. A character in a Victor Hugo play declares: '*Le vent qui vient à travers la montagne me rendra fou*' – 'the wind that comes across the mountain will drive me mad' – and the Garcia Marquez story 'Tramontana' also deals with a young boy marked by the mysterious effects of this wind.

I had reached the end of my tether after only a few hours. The Captain was on deck, struggling with the helm, when I stumbled my way up to him, screaming at him above the noise of the wind to get me out of this.

I was almost hysterical yet he remained strangely calm.

'Don't you think I would if I could?'

I gazed about me at black skies stabbed by forked lightning. It seemed as if we were the only boat at sea and I was seized by a kind of helplessness I hadn't felt for a very long time. For several more hours there was nothing I could do but cling to the hope that we would ride out the storm until at last, by some miracle, the Captain was steering us out of the wind and into safety.

The following morning, we were anchored in a sheltered bay when we saw another boat limping in towards us. Its prow was shattered and the safety rail had gone. When it drew in alongside us we took on board a young couple and their baby. They were exhausted and shivering with shock. As I made them something to eat they marvelled over how we had escaped the storm unscathed. We insisted they spend the night in the dry cabin of the *Golden Sunset*. As they slept I asked the Captain, 'How could you not be scared of the storm?'

He tells me the truth now, with no hint of bravado. 'I was as terrified as you.' He looks at me and then says something I will always remember. 'After a while, you get tired of being scared.'

Perhaps my friends were right and I was running away from reality, seeking a cure for my heartache in far-flung ports. When I did manage to write, it was helping me to make sense of things. I now knew that wherever I went, I brought all my emotional baggage with me. Soon I came to realise that I wasn't travelling but wandering.

Chapter Twelve

A New Tack

On 3 June 1988, I drank a toast to Sarah Louise and wished her all the happiness in the world as she embarked on her adult life. It was eighteen years to the day since I had given birth at the Salvation Army Mothers' Hospital in Hackney. If my daughter had been told she was adopted she would almost certainly know that she now had a right to her original birth certificate. Sitting in the Mediterranean sunshine, I was taken back to another hot afternoon, to a registrar visiting a hospital ward, Martin and I deciding on a name for our baby and then adding our own. Would Sarah Louise ever read that indelible record?

Would she ever seek us out? Or would I live all my days waiting for her, as I had waited for a photograph that never arrived?

I had always known that my daughter was out there somewhere, in the background, but the thought that she might appear in my life at any moment from now on made me conscious that I needed to take stock. I was aware that I'd never really stretched myself career-wise but, having spent so long bobbing around on a boat, I was also beginning to feel under-used, as though I was wasting any small talent I might have. If I needed an example of what might happen if I didn't get my act together, I had one right in front of me: the Captain was now almost fifty and still had no real plans to do anything with his life but sail. I had a wider sense, too, that the times were moving on without me and saw evidence of that when I went back to England and in the Brits who arrived on the islands clutching Filofaxes and staggering under the weight of the early portable phones. I felt that if I stayed on that boat much longer there would be no going back to London.

Not long after raising my glass to Sarah Louise, I met another Julie, known as Jools, an English girl in her late twenties who was holidaying alone in Menorca. She lived in London and it transpired that we had a mutual friend in Richard, who had first suggested that the Captain and I brought the boat to Ciudadella. Richard was also a friend of the owner of the countryside villa where she was staying. Small world. Jools and I took off to a pizzeria one evening and got on like a house on fire.

The waiter brought our pizzas and placed them before us with a flourish, smiling, 'Julie *la rubia*… y Julie *la negra*.' For fair Julie and dark Julie. Over our meal I found myself confiding to Jools that if I didn't take on a new challenge soon I'd probably go mad, like a dog left out too long in the sun. She told me about her career as a commercials producer and I mentioned that I'd worked in radio drama before taking to the seas. Then, out of the blue, she offered me a job.

Jools suggested I might just fit into a new sideline to her business. She and her two partners had recently set up a publishing venture, a directory of services and personnel for the commercials industry, and they needed someone sparky and outgoing to sell advertising space in it. Work would start on the directory in September and it would be off to press by the following May, which would leave me free to spend the summer months on the boat. What did I think?

Her timing couldn't have been better. It was the ideal solution.

The Captain was less enamoured of the idea. He took the news despondently, finding it hard to understand why anyone would want to go back and live in London. But we knew that coming with me was never going to be an option for him, and he accepted that remaining aboard the *Golden Sunset* wasn't working for me. At Mahón airport we bade each other a tearful farewell, until the next voyage, and I moved back into my room at the Westy in Notting Hill.

It was something of a culture shock. Although I had been returning to London every so often, I hadn't adjusted to the changing times on a day-to-day basis.

Since all my clothes dated back to 1984 or 1985, I looked, and felt, like a recently released prisoner. Having always been a hippy at heart, I found I'd been parachuted into the yuppy era.

I'd spent my youth rejecting money-based values, aware that there had always been long-haired entrepreneurs around masquerading as hippy types – Richard Branson, for example. We had a derogatory word to describe them: breadheads. But suddenly it was OK to be a breadhead. Thatcherism was at its height and 'Greed is good', the motto of the ruthless Gordon Gekko in the Oscar-winning film *Wall Street*, released the previous year, seemed to have taken root in the national consciousness. I remembered the warning of another character in that movie, 'Good things take time', but no one wanted to hear that. It was all about the fast buck, cruising in your sleek BMW with the receiver of your car phone clamped to your ear, champagne flowing in City bars. Power dressing and big hair were the order of the day for the new generation of go-getting young women, who went around with their jacket sleeves rolled up to the elbow, ready for action. And here I was starting work in advertising, one of the industries that most typified these materialistic values.

I hated the trend for conspicuous displays of wealth and the clutter of consumerism. The wretched Filofaxes touted by Jools and her partners in my new office at the top end of Ladbroke Grove were a particular *bête noire*, to their amusement. As far as I was concerned it

was nothing more than a glorified diary, designed to convey the impression that its owner's life was so frantically busy every detail and appointment had to be catalogued, compartmentalised and at hand every minute of every day. I insisted on a small diary from Woolworth's.

For the first time in my life, I heard myself sounding reactionary and even a little bitter. When mobile phones became more compact and more widely available, poor, dear Seb, who loved to be in the vanguard of fashion, got an earful.

'I think I'll get one of these new mobile phones,' he mused.

'Are you joking?' I snapped. 'They're for posers! There's even a stall down Portobello market selling rubber ones called phoney phones. Save yourself a few quid and buy one of those instead. It's just a fad. People will get tired of those things soon.'

To this day I don't have a mobile phone but I'm still waiting for everyone else to get tired of them.

Notting Hill, too, had changed in my absence. The bedsit population and the West Indians were being replaced by yuppies and the area was becoming a magnet for media types. Almost overnight, it seemed, the ironmongery shop vanished, the post office was transformed into a frighteningly expensive florist's and a Tom Conran deli opened up next door to it. Soon Beach Blanket Babylon would appear on Ledbury Road along with the host of other trendy restaurants springing up on Portobello Road. My Notting Hill friends, mostly hippies who had lived there for years, shook their heads in dismay. 'I feel like a bison on the North American plains when the settlers came,' grumbled one girlfriend. 'About to become extinct.' The Westy began to seem like the last bastion of a simpler, more bohemian life.

Late on a Saturday night, after a crowd had dropped into the Westy, sunk a few too many drinks and were busy dancing around the sitting room with Seb's plastic fruit on their heads like deranged Carmen Mirandas, he would whisper to me, 'What would we do if your daughter knocked on the door now?' I would laugh, but comments like that reinforced the sense I had that this freewheeling lifestyle – no proper home, no rent, no responsibilities – was hardly appropriate to my age, not to mention what a daughter might expect of her long-lost birth mother.

Still, I was heading in the right direction by having a proper job, and for once in my life I was being well paid. Jools and her partners, Debbie and Tina, were all younger than me by four or five years. Jools was a tomboy, a witty practical joker though always efficient when it came to work. Tina was stylish, beautiful and had a steely ambition; Debbie an eccentric *bon viveur* with a penchant for collecting lame ducks. They were all generous to a fault and they all worked hard and played hard. At six o'clock every evening they took turns to strike a metal radiator – bong! – to signal that

it was time for our first vodka and tonic of the evening.
There was always more than one.

All commercials producers themselves, they had
spotted an information gap in their own market and
had filled it with their directory, which was called *The
Knowledge*. For £50 a copy, they offered listings of the
kinds of contacts to be found in their Filofaxes. I was
to sell advertising space in the new edition to the
companies and crew who were included in the directory
– anything from a little box ad at £200 to a front cover
at £2,000.

The girls decided I needed transport and bought me
a car, a green second-hand Renault 5 with matching
scatter cushions on the back seat. The only hitch was I
had never got round to learning to drive. I had to do so
now. I was thirty-five years old and my instructor,
Andy, wondered why I hadn't had lessons as a teenager.
I told him I'd had other things on my mind. As we
spent morning after morning kangarooing up and
down Kensington High Street, I couldn't help wondering whether Sarah Louise was also struggling to
remember 'Mirror, Signal, Manoeuvre' or making a
hash of a three-point turn. Or perhaps she had been
given driving lessons the moment she turned seven-
teen, and was even now whizzing confidently past me
to wherever she called home.

To Andy's astonishment, I passed my driving test
first time and set off to introduce *The Knowledge* to
anyone in the business who might be interested in

advertising in it. I got to meet lots of new people, from studio bosses to location chefs. I loved the social side of my job, and getting to visit professionals on site gave me a good overview of the industry and how its various elements fitted together, but eventually I found I sold more space by just staying in the office and making phone calls. I kept index cards to jog my memory. If someone told me they'd broken their leg skiing, for example, when I rang back in six weeks I would check the card and remember to ask, 'How's the leg?' It wasn't sales patter, just common courtesy, and besides, I was genuinely interested in the answer. I was making new friends among my customers as well as with my bosses.

Having been thrown into the deep end at the Knowledge Production Company, I was beginning to swim. Jools, Debbie and Tina were all single career girls, though Tina was engaged, to a successful showbiz lawyer. They were fearless: none of them knew the meaning of the word no. The main part of their business was providing production services for overseas companies, particularly in the US, who found it cheaper to make their ads in the UK. Operating to extremely tight deadlines, often with huge sums of money at stake, the girls would manage the seemingly impossible time and again in the course of a two-day shoot – finding some elusive prop or dealing with a logistical or casting problem that could have halted a production at a stroke. It was incredibly stressful work but they never gave up. In fact they seemed to thrive on it. I was learning a lot from them about perseverance and about the importance of setting yourself goals and achieving them. The girls were also encouraging me to think positively about what I might be able to achieve for myself.

Looking back, I was probably carrying with me an unacknowledged and only half-percived sense of having underachieved at school and even, to some extent, at university. Now, albeit belatedly, the happy hippy was compensating for that, and for the years spent on the boat doing very little, by working extra hard and pushing herself, perhaps for the first time ever.

I was still uncomfortable with some of the sums of money swilling around the industry but I couldn't shout too loudly as I was a part of it myself now, and it was paying me a good salary. When I'd taken the job, the girls had asked me whether I'd like to buy into the business as a shareholder with my first year's commission, but I'd told them I was happier just working for my wages without the extra responsibility such an investment would imply. It was a short-sighted decision, as accepting that offer would have made me a lot of money when they sold the company. But I'd never been interested in accumulating money for the sake of it. To me a good job was one that afforded me plenty of time off to do something more important, and more enjoyable, like my writing.

In the meantime, I was coming to recognise that my childless motherhood was an essential part of me. It had helped to make me into the person I was and hiding it from those who cared about me was not good for me or for my relationships with them. To have done so would have been to perpetuate the damaging family history of keeping secrets I had always so regretted. My oldest and closest friends had known about Sarah Louise for years. Jools, Tina, Debbie and I were now very close, too, sharing each other's ups and downs, so one evening I told them about her. I studied their faces, trying to gauge their reactions, which I interpreted as a mixture of shock, sympathy and perhaps even horror at the idea that someone they thought they knew so well had been living with this private tragedy all along. It broke down any remaining barriers between us, and that was the way it needed to be.

The girls were very supportive of me in this, as they were in everything else. Tina was very keen to get into drama and, knowing that I wrote short stories, she mentioned to me that she'd heard Channel 4 were launching a scheme to bring short films by new writers and directors to the screen. She suggested I should try to adapt one of my stories as a short film script. The films would be given proper budgets and would have to be made to a professional standard, so submissions would be accepted only from bona fide production companies. But that was no problem: we could enter a proposal from the Knowledge Production Company. It would be a potential opportunity for her to produce a first drama piece, too.

I did try to rework a story that seemed to lend itself to film but I wasn't happy with the result and put the script to one side. I never seemed to have enough spare time to complete a writing project. I had almost forgotten all about the Channel 4 scheme until a friend, Howard Greenberg, over on a visit from New York, told me an amusing anecdote about his grandfather's funeral. His story gave me another idea.

Inspired, I set to work, producing a twelve-minute script called *Geh Kinde Geh*, Yiddish for 'go child go'. The main character was Stella, a possessive Jewish mother keen to use the occasion of a family funeral to marry off her gay son to the daughter of an old friend. As Stella tries to teach her prospective daughter-in-law to make *latkes*, potato pancakes, the exasperated girl tells her that Howard will have problems loving any woman as much as he loves his mother. Stella is angrily dismissive. 'What do you know about love? What d'you know about *latkes*?'

Amid the jokes about blinkered denial and dysfunctional family life lay the poignant story of a mother's love and ambition for her child. Towards the end of the script, a little girl turns up unexpectedly on the doorstep, revealing herself to be the daughter of the dead family member.

My intention had been simply to write an entertaining black comedy but, in many ways, it was as though the story had written itself. Time was passing. Sarah Louise was nineteen now, and the information she would have needed to trace me had been available to her for a whole year. Perhaps I had been driven to write the fictional happy ending that seemed to be evading me in real life.

Tina submitted *Geh Kinde Geh* to Channel 4 and in due course she received a standard rejection letter – huge number of applications, you have been unlucky this time, the usual thing. We were both disappointed, though not surprised. We were well aware that there had been a lot of entries: just about every production company had submitted something, including commercials outfits like ours trying to get into drama. Even Seb had reworked a film-school script and sent it in. When we had a rejection letter and he didn't, he thought he might be in with a chance.

Then, suddenly, everything was turned on its head. Tina was puzzled to receive a phone call from Channel 4 inviting her to a production meeting for *Geh Kinde Geh*. She explained that they must have made a mistake: our project had been rejected weeks before. Channel 4 said they would check the situation and ring her straight back. When they did I was looking at her intently from my desk, trying to work out from each nod or shake of her head whether the news was good or bad.

Tina put down the phone, her face glum. 'Well, there was definitely a mistake.'

'Too bad.' I tried not to seem too crushed.

A smile spread slowly across her features as she stood up and walked over to my desk. 'They said if a rejection letter was sent out, *that* was the mistake. They've always wanted to make this film!'

We both burst out laughing and hugged one another.

A week or two later, Seb's script was rejected. I knew how disappointed he must be and it was awkward for both of us as we could neither celebrate together nor commiserate with each other. And neither of us needed reminding that he was the professional and I was the amateur. On one slightly tense evening, a rather camp friend of ours fussed around us both. 'Oh, my!' he declared. 'I can see this is going to be like Joe Orton and Ken Halliwell. Before long one of you is going to end up with your head stoved in!'

Seb and I both laughed, but rather hollowly.

Tina went to the production meeting with Channel 4 and British Screen, their partners in the project, and returned with the news that we were being given a budget of over £90,000 to shoot *Geh Kinde Geh*. This seemed to me an astronomical sum until Tina explained that as the drama was to be handled by Channel 4's film company, Film Four, we would have to shoot not on videotape but on expensive 35mm film. It was going to be just like a real movie. She set about hiring a director and settled on Crispin Reece. Although he had made only one film of his own, another short, an impressive CV as first or second assistant director – which included big features like *Clockwise*, *The Whistle Blower* and the

James Bond movie *The Living Daylights* – testified to plenty of shooting experience at a high level.

The first thing Crispin did for us was to borrow a Bond office at Eon Productions, where we auditioned the potential cast. In an impressive room at Pinewood Studios, I sat in a green leather-backed chair that had perhaps once been occupied by Cubby Broccoli himself and met actors I had only seen previously on stage and TV. They read speeches from the script and offered new and very interesting interpretations of the characters I had written. Tina, Crispin and I made our decisions. Bernard Spear took the part of Stella's long-suffering husband. A prolific actor, he had appeared in Hollywood films like *Chitty Chitty Bang Bang*, and *Yentl* with Barbra Streisand, on stage, notably in David Mamet's *The Duck Variations*, and had a list of television credits as long as your arm, ranging from *The Likely Lads* to *The Bar Mitzvah Boy*.

As Stella, I had always wanted Maria Charles, and I managed to get my wish. I had seen her on television playing Maureen Lipman's mother in the 1980s sitcom *Agony* and I felt she was perfect for the role of a well-meaning, slightly neurotic middle-aged woman trying to exert control over a chaotic household. In some ways she reminded me of my mother.

On the first day of shooting I was staggered to find so many people gathered on set – directors, sound engineers, crane operators, hairdressers and make-up assistants – all milling about busily. I must have looked staggered, too, because a stuntman leaned in to me and whispered encouragingly, 'They wouldn't be here if it weren't for you.' I allowed myself to believe that everything in my life was slotting into place. Or almost everything.

I had no idea that shooting a film, especially a short one, could prove such long and arduous work. We were up at dawn and didn't get to bed until very late. Overnight Crispin would be viewing rushes of the previous day's filming and often he had to reorganise the following day's shoot to meet our deadlines. While I'd been writing the script I hadn't thought much about the practical difficulties of filming what was on the page. One short scene consisted of a row of undertakers being distracted from their duties by an attractive woman walking her dog. What could be simpler? But it meant casting a dog and we didn't have enough left in our budget for an animal-handler.

When I discovered this, I decided that my neighbour's dog might fit the bill. I wasn't sure what breed he was – he looked like a larger version of a chocolate Labrador – but he seemed intelligent and was always friendly when we met in the street. I put my proposition to my neighbour but he told me he couldn't bring the dog to the set on the scheduled day because he was going to be out of town. However, since he could see that the dog and I got along, the promise of a small financial contribution was enough to secure his agreement to entrust his pooch to me.

I duly arrived at the shoot with Rocky the Rottweiler in tow.

Until that point, I hadn't been aware of the dog's true breed, and even if I had, I'd have thought nothing of it as I had no idea that Rottweilers could be dangerous. Although Rocky had always been perfectly behaved when I'd bumped into him with his owner, on set he seemed to be a different dog entirely. Any member of the crew attempting a pace faster than a brisk walk was chased and mown down. Rocky growled when petted and refused to co-operate with any of the director's instructions. A simple visual joke was becoming a logistical nightmare. But I had learned at the feet of the masters, the indefatigable trio of Tina, Jools and Debbie, and 'impossible' was not a word in their vocabulary. I racked my brains until I hit upon a solution: the catering van. After a brief conversation with our location chef, thirty sausages were quickly fried up and I stuffed them in my jacket pockets. Rocky now followed me wherever I went and performed all of his tasks beautifully, and on cue. I had a new best friend for the price of some pork chipolatas.

Within weeks the film was not only in the can, it had been edited and was ready to be shown at a preview theatre in London to an audience of cast, crew and family members. Since I didn't have any close family, I brought plenty of friends and Mark's parents. As the credits flashed up on the screen I couldn't help but wonder if, when the film was finally shown on television, my nearest blood relative might see it and recognise my name. But at that stage I still had no idea whether Sarah Louise even knew my name.

Chapter Thirteen

18 Jermyn Street

When *Geh Kinde Geh* was transmitted on Channel 4, it received good reviews. Tina and I were thrilled. In the girls' eyes, I was now a fully fledged writer. A month or so earlier, I had been setting off for a meeting somewhere with Tina. She'd taken one look at me, said, 'I can't go to an important meeting with you carrying your stuff in a Tesco bag,' and lent me a stylish Nicole Farhi store bag in which to hide it. Primed not to let her down, en route to a more recent appointment, I had been appalled to discover a large hole spreading out from under the arm of my jumper.

'What am I going to *do*?'

'That's all right, Julie,' she soothed. 'You're a writer. You can wear whatever you like.'

There had, it seemed, been a shift in my identity. Now I could look the part and be as bohemian and scruffy as I wanted.

After the Channel 4 broadcast there was no special phone call from my daughter and no letter in the post. By this time she was twenty, and I had to face the fact that, even if she had seen the film, in all probability my name meant nothing to her. Somebody else did get in touch, though not because he had seen *Geh Kinde Geh*. It had been nearly two years since I'd left the Captain on the *Golden Sunset* and returned to London. In the interim he had written and phoned occasionally. I had been back to Menorca on holiday but not to sail with him, though he had remained in southern Spain, seduced by the cheap booze and low mooring fees. Now, ready to 'screw the nut', he was planning to take another long sea voyage. He asked me if I would go with him.

I was torn. The long bridge that stretched between the Captain and me had grown more rickety with time. Part of me wanted to flee back across it before it collapsed altogether; to throw a few things in a bag, leave the rat race behind me and return to the uncomplicated freedom of the sea. But I knew I had now laid the foundations of something more solid on my side of the bridge. It was almost as if I were being tested: I wanted to stay in London, to build a settled life for myself and to carry on writing, but did I have what it took to achieve that? For my own sake, I had to give it a go.

I would keep in intermittent contact with the Captain over the years and sadly, my fears about his laissez-faire

approach to making a living from his boat, the reposi-
tory of everything he had, proved well founded. As his
funds dwindled, he kept having to downsize, and before
long he had been forced to trade the fifty-foot *Golden
Sunset* for a twenty-footer. I lent him some money at
one stage, all of which he faithfully paid back, but it
was never going to be enough to stop the rot. He would
eventually end his days in the Med without, as far as I
know, ever making the ultimate voyage of his dreams.
But I prefer to picture him toasting the summer solstice
with aquavit as fireworks light up the nightless sky
over a Norwegian fjord, and to think of him fearlessly
steering his beloved boat across the open seas for all
time.

Meanwhile, I had temporarily moved out of the
Westy, which had become somewhat cramped owing to
an influx of Annie's visitors, to house-sit for some
people who were going away on a long holiday. On
their return I had been asked to do the same for other
friends. Over a period of six months I had become a
land gypsy, 'caretaking' homes in the contrasting areas
of Holland Park and Stoke Newington. It had been fun
for a while but I was growing tired of packing everything I owned into the boot of my little car and driving
it to another part of London like a displaced Beverly
Hillbilly.

I was getting older, and finally burning my boats
with the Captain highlighted my awareness of my
single status. I would have liked a lasting relationship

with a nice man but by now I knew that most prospective partners would probably want a family. I still didn't
feel able to cope with that after losing the child to
whom I'd given birth – I still wasn't even comfortable
holding other women's newborn babies. Mr Right
would have to be a truly special person to take on the
chaos of my life and guide me out of the cul-de-sac I'd
taken, the street marked 'No kids'. I couldn't see a way
out of it on my own. Perhaps my hormones were
putting me under some pressure, though my biological
clock was more like a cuckoo clock, with the bird inside
awaiting its cue to spring out and squawk: 'Too late!'

I needed to grab my life by the scruff of the neck
and build on the start I'd been given in screenwriting.
Virginia Woolf once said that a woman must have
money and a room of her own if she was to write
fiction. I made a decision. A few weeks after the
Captain's phone call, I wrote a letter of application to
the Church Commissioners' Housing Association in
Peckham, close to where my old friend Mark, now back
in the UK, had bought a flat. He warned me that housing association flats in the area were few and far
between and, remembering how my parents had waited
for the best part of twenty years to be rehoused, I
didn't hold out much hope. But if I didn't apply I'd have
no hope at all, so I reasoned it was worth a try.

To my amazement, it wasn't long before I learned I
was at the top of the Church Commissioners' list and
that a small, one-bedroomed, ground-floor flat just off

the Walworth Road was about to become available to rent.

Would I like to take it? Of course I would.

The tiny flat in Merrow Street, south-east London, was in a grim condition. An old lady had died there: a terrible smell lingered everywhere and there were dark stains on the bedroom floorboards. I was earning enough to cover the rent and furnish the place but there was nothing left over for extras so I would just need to roll up my sleeves and try to sort it out myself.

When friends came to have a look at the place I could see they were struggling to find something nice to say about it. Jaws dropped when I cheerfully announced that I'd taken a week off work to make it habitable, but I was confident I could manage it. They rolled up their sleeves, too, and lent a hand. Even casual acquaintances gave up their time to help me. Bryony, an out-of-work commercials producer, spent days with me steaming off years of filthy wallpaper and gloss paint from every wall and ceiling. She hung fresh wallpaper, I sanded and sealed floorboards, the caretaker knocked out a fireplace for me and I plastered the cracks with my bare hands. Having led the life of a gypsy on land and sea for so long, I didn't own as much as a knife and fork, but several late-night trips to Ikea remedied that.

By the Sunday night I was sitting back and surveying my newly refurbished home with satisfaction. Only the small bathroom remained to be decorated, but I

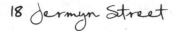

wasn't too bothered about that and it wouldn't take long. I was due back at work the next day, but first I had one more thing to do in the morning to complete my fresh start – and it took precedence over the bathroom. I had to pluck up the courage to see someone about pursuing my writing career.

Since making *Geh Kinde Geh*, I'd been given a lot of encouragement by Adrian Hodges who, as development executive of British Screen, had pushed to get my film made. Afterwards he had continued to support me with help and advice, nominating me for a residential writers' course in Devon. As well as teaching me more about the craft and the business of writing, the course had given me a welcome opportunity to meet other new writers. On the last day, some of us exchanged telephone numbers, promising to stay in touch. One novelist, a young American called Jon Fink, asked me if I'd thought about getting an agent. It wasn't the first time this had been suggested to me. Adrian had talked about it too, recommending someone called Michelle Kass at Hatton & Baker.

I hadn't acted on Adrian's advice, feeling unsure and apprehensive about what an agent might expect of me, but now, miles from London in the Devon countryside, someone from another country was giving me the same name. And he didn't just mention the name in passing, he actually took my address book from my hand and insisted on scribbling down her phone number. 'Call her,' he said. 'I think you'll get along.'

With Michelle practically handed to me on a plate, I felt braver. On my return from Devon I had phoned her office and had been asked to send in some samples of my work. I'd duly posted off *Geh Kinde Geh*, along with another idea for a screenplay. A few days later, someone from Hatton & Baker had called to arrange an appointment for me to go in and talk to Michelle.

I wasn't quite sure what to wear that morning. In the end I opted for a long black coat over a jumper and jeans, tied back my long hair and walked into the bathroom to put on some lipstick.

I thought back to the time my parents had been given their fresh start in a council maisonette. I'd spoiled that for them, and for myself, by moving into our new home concealing a teenage pregnancy that would shock them to the core. The whole experience had continued to reverberate throughout my own life but now it seemed as though I was being offered a second chance to steady that life, perhaps even to shape it into the one I should always have been leading – if only I had succeeded in finding the mould a bit sooner.

A small mirror hung perilously from the bathroom wall. I would get around to sorting out this bathroom soon, but for now I considered I'd achieved quite a lot in the past week. Having my own home for the first time in years, I was no longer at sea, in any sense of the word. I felt I was finally putting down roots in what the Captain would have described as a 'shore station'.

Checking my make-up, I smiled at the memory of Seb's recurring question on mad, drunken Saturday nights at the Westy. 'What would we do if your daughter knocked on the door now?' Well, if Sarah Louise knocked on the door now, I was ready for her at last. Maybe my home wasn't a palace but my life was in order and I was leading it in a more focused way than I probably ever had before.

In fact, I thought suddenly as I gazed at my reflection in the bathroom mirror, now would be the very best time for my daughter to come and find me.

I picked up my bag and left for my appointment in town.

It was the morning of Monday 5 November 1990. I took the tube to Piccadilly Circus and made my way to Jermyn Street. I was about as far 'up West' as a number 8 bus from my old home in Mile End could possibly have taken me. All I had known about it then, courtesy of my father, was that Sir Isaac Newton had lived here during his time as warden of the Royal Mint. It was more famous as the street where the wealthy man-about-town traditionally purchased his shirts. Hatton & Baker's neighbours in this unambiguously upper-crust and masculine milieu included cigar shops, shoe and bootmakers, the barber George F. Trumper and Tramp nightclub, as well as the quality shirtmakers, such as Turnbull & Asser, for which it was renowned. You could almost smell the expensive cologne, fine leather and puffs of Havana smoke.

I paused outside number 18 and asked myself what on earth I was doing here. I wasn't even sure what an agent did, let alone what an agent might want me to do. What I did know, because I had looked them up, was that Hatton & Baker represented a long list of famous names. On their client list was the actor Richard Harris, whom I remembered especially for his performance in the 1963 masterpiece *This Sporting Life*. I had seen this film as a child, but Harris was still working prolifically – he would soon go on to play Dumbledore in the Harry Potter films. They also looked after Leo McKern of *Rumpole of the Bailey*, one of my favourite television shows, and Leslie Phillips, whose portrayal of a hapless sub-lieutenant in *The Navy Lark* I'd so enjoyed listening to with my parents in the 1960s. There were many directors, too, including Nicholas Roeg, who had made the unforgettably mysterious feature film *Don't Look Now*, set in Venice and starring Julie Christie.

All I had to offer were some sketchy ideas for future projects and the first draft of a film script for a romantic comedy called *Lucky Break*. Inspired by Elizabeth Ashley's incongruous visit to the Westy, this featured a character, based on Seb, who takes advantage of the unexpected arrival of a Hollywood star at his dilapidated house in Notting Hill to try to rescue his floundering acting career.

At the heart of the story was the old screwball comedy idea of a clash of two contrasting worlds leading, ultimately, to love. A few development producers had read the script, including Adrian Hodges. He had been supportive, as ever, but the general view was that the idea was too far-fetched. Almost a decade later, Richard Curtis's film *Notting Hill* was to meet with box-office success. It wasn't connected in any way to my script which, by then, I had long since abandoned. No one had really believed me when I had told them my story was based on fact. My life at the Westy certainly had been stranger than fiction.

I wondered now whether, if I had started writing earlier or stuck with it after I left college, I might by this time be further established in a proper career. But this was just wishful thinking. I knew that, however long you worked at it, with writing there were no guarantees. In many ways, *Geh Kinde Geh* had been my own 'lucky break'.

Looking at the door of 18 Jermyn Street, I was beginning to question whether I might be pushing that luck by even coming here. In short, I was suffering a serious loss of nerve. In an effort to muster my courage, I took a deep breath and made a quick mental inventory of all the events that had brought me to this office. Two unrelated people had urged me to call Michelle Kass; one had even written her name and number in my address book. I had spent my entire life either reading or writing works of fiction and had recently been fortunate enough to have a little film made. The girls at work, with irrepressible optimism, had convinced me that all things were possible. Now was not the time to start disputing that. Besides, what was the worst that could happen? Taking another deep breath, I rang the bell.

A few moments later, I was shown into Michelle's office. She was, I would later learn, the youngest partner at Hatton & Baker. She immediately got to her feet to shake my hand, a friendly, approachable woman a few years younger than me with tight, dark curls that brought to mind my far-off experiences with the straightening tongs. Michelle, however, wore her curly hair with confidence. I would have been put at my ease straight away had I not been distracted by an extra-ordinary machine that was sitting on her desk, a real Heath Robinson contraption. I couldn't imagine what its function might be, and once it had caught my eye I found it hard to ignore.

Michelle saw me looking at it.

'It's a milk expresser. The Rolls-Royce of its kind,' she explained. 'I'm renting it from the National Child-birth Trust.'

She told me that it was helping to solve one of the dilemmas of the modern working mum. She had a demanding job and needed to be back in the office fairly soon after giving birth to her baby son, but at the same time she wanted to breastfeed him for the first six months of his life.

This explanation proved to be something of an ice-breaker, which was just as well, as the milk expresser wasn't going anywhere. It remained between us on

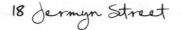

Michelle's desk, reminding me of the flow of my own milk twenty years before, leaking on to a tie-dye dress at the Hackney Wick dog track. Once coffee had been brought, Michelle and I settled down to discuss the purpose of my visit. We talked through my own few projects, our conversation ranging over films, plays and novels we had both enjoyed and some we hadn't.

Michelle had strong opinions, a keen sense of humour and a welcome curiosity about me and my work. We laughed a lot and I felt comfortable in her company. Finally, she asked if I had read any short stories by Elizabeth Taylor – not the Hollywood actress, but the English novelist. I had to admit that I hadn't. We chatted on as we finished our coffee. Before I left, Michelle agreed to take me on as a client and handed me a paperback collection of short stories, *The Blush*, recommending that I read one in particular.

As I stepped out on to Jermyn Street, I felt encouraged. It had been a brief meeting, but it was long enough for me to know that I liked Michelle and to feel that we had a good rapport. On the busy platform at Piccadilly Circus tube station, I jostled with commuters, shoppers and tourists before finally wrestling my way on to a train. I was pleased to be able to get a seat, because I wanted to take a proper look at the book she had given me. Reaching into my bag, I pulled out the paperback and thumbed through it until I found the story she had mentioned. It was entitled 'Perhaps a

Family Failing'. Before settling down to read it, I allowed myself the thought that maybe, just maybe, something might come of this.

Chapter Fourteen

Three O'Clock at the Pagoda

I was in my office the next day when the call came through.

It was Michelle. I could tell instantly from the tone of her voice that something was wrong. At our meeting she had been self-assured, businesslike in a friendly way. Not intimidating, but definitely a woman in control. Today her voice was awkward, uncertain, tight with worry. 'I'm not sure I'm doing the right thing,' she began. 'But there's something I feel I have to tell you.'

I automatically assumed that she had reconsidered and decided against taking me on. Even that didn't seem to explain the dramatic difference in mood: as an agent, she must have been used to letting people down gently. But I'd only met her once – what else could it be? I braced myself for disappointment and told her not to worry, whatever it was she had to say, I would be

OK with it. There was a long pause before she spoke again.

Choosing her words very carefully, she began to recount how, earlier that day, she had asked a young secretary to come into her office and take some dictation. The girl worked for another agent at Hatton & Baker but was helping out because Michelle's own secretary was away. It had been Michelle's intention to send on a copy of my *Geh Kinde Geh* script to her brother, Harvey, a film producer, but she didn't get that far. While dictating a note to him, she had handed the script to the secretary, indicating that it was accompany the letter.

Suddenly, the girl had put down her pen and turned white as a sheet.

Michelle paused for a moment. 'It was the same girl who brought us coffee yesterday,' Michelle went on. 'Do you remember her? Because I'm sure I introduced you.'

I racked my brains, but I couldn't remember. Surely I would have made eye contact, smiled, said I was pleased to meet her? Somebody had certainly brought us coffee but she had set it down on the desk and disappeared quickly: a brief and inconsequential encounter, like passing a stranger on the stairs. Perhaps at that moment I had been put off my stroke by the milk expresser. I had to confess I had no recollection of being introduced to anyone in the office.

Michelle continued her story. 'I knew none of this until today. But just a couple of hours ago this girl confided to me that she had been adopted as a baby.'

I listened, becoming curious now.

'A while ago she gained access to her birth certificate, and from that she learned the name of her mother. The name she recognised on a script I passed to her this morning. Julie Wassmer.'

The buzz of the busy office, phones ringing, keyboards tapping, the low murmur of voices, every sound seems suddenly to recede, as if someone is turning down the volume on the room. All I can hear now is the voice on the other end of the line.

'She's twenty years old,' Michelle is saying. 'And her name is Sara. Does this mean anything to you?'

Silence now, a numbing hiatus as I attempt to rationalise what is happening. I know Michelle is waiting for a response. I try to speak but nothing comes out.

Michelle fills the silence, a tremor in her voice. 'She's waiting in the other office right now. But I'm alone, the door is closed, and whatever you say can stay between us.'

I gasp, brought back to life. I hear myself replying: 'Tell her it's me.'

There is another pause as Michelle takes this in. Before she can speak again, I say that I will have to call her back. I put down the receiver.

How many times in my life had I used the word 'stunned'? I had written it in a thousand descriptions without ever really understanding the full force of its meaning – until now. 'To render unconscious by a blow;

to stupefy or daze.' It was the right word. I was stunned.

On the other side of the desk, my new assistant, Vicky, was on the phone. I could see her lips moving but what she was saying was of no consequence to me. I began to act without thinking. Instead of dialling Michelle's number I got up from my chair, crossed the office floor and picked up my coat from its hook.

Debbie was coming downstairs from the mezzanine floor behind me when she saw me making for the door. Her voice stopped me in my tracks.

'Where are you off to?'

I looked back at her. Strangely calm, I told her exactly what I had just heard on the phone.

Debbie stared at me, open-mouthed, for several long seconds.

'Fifty-five million people in Britain and your agent's secretary turns out to be your long-lost daughter?'

I had no answer. My body, moving of its own accord, was drawing me towards the door. 'I have to go to her, Debbie.'

By now she had registered that I was in shock. That I was behaving like the victim of an air crash asking whether the luggage will follow on before sliding out of the emergency exit.

'No,' she said. 'Hold on.'

She hurried back up to the mezzanine floor where Jools and Tina were working. A moment later they were all coming down, high heels clacking on the metal stairs. They ushered me off to the only place where it was possible to have a private discussion: the ladies' room.

All four of us squashed into the office loo, where the girls persuaded me that I needed to take time to think through how I should handle the situation. Theories and suggestions bounced off the tiled walls. Chance encounters like this simply didn't happen, they said, and there wasn't a precedent for dealing with them. I might do terrible damage if I went charging in like a bull in a china shop. People searched for years to find each other, and when they did, they were given counselling before they met. Someone decided that perhaps that should be the next step. I leaned back against the washbasin, dazed, while the girls took over. Tina was nominated to speak to Michelle and work was suspended while they addressed the crisis.

We went back into the office and, returning to my desk, I made a point of explaining to Vicky what had just happened. I knew she wouldn't have had a clue what was going on and I didn't want her to think that we had squeezed into the toilet to discuss her. Once I had finished my story, she stretched out her arm across my desk. 'Look,' she said. Every fine, pale hair on her forearm was standing on end.

The girls made an appointment for me at the Post-Adoption Centre, a charity that provided counselling and support to all parties affected by the adoption process. Michelle called Tina back with the news that Sara, having received similar advice at her workplace, was going to approach Norcap, another support agency, with which she had been in touch before in her teenage years. Everyone agreed that the professionals would know how best to cope with an event like this. They would tell us what we should do.

The girls encouraged me to stick to the plans I already had for the evening, and so I went out for dinner with Jools and some friends and business associates as had been arranged. We met up in a restaurant in North London. It was the night after Bonfire Night and the sky was still filled with the customary multi-coloured explosions. My face was a mask of calmness and capability but the news had yet to sink in. All I could think about was that somewhere, in some other part of London, my baby girl was out there – grown up now, but there were surely going to be emotional fireworks for her, too.

After dinner, I took up an offer from friends to stay overnight with them in Stoke Newington. When I woke up in the early hours of the morning I was trembling, suffering from delayed shock. I was desperate to communicate with Sara. I made myself a cup of hot, sweet tea, sat down and wrote her a long letter explaining the circumstances of her birth. I forced myself to revisit all the details of my concealed pregnancy. As I wrote I began to weep for my lost child. I wept in a visceral way, a way in which I had never been able to cry for her in twenty years. It felt as if layer upon layer of scar tissue was being stripped away, exposing a wound that had never healed. Fireworks were still banging and fizzing outside. Or was it fallout from the final, cataclysmic collision of my two worlds?

There was no denial now, and nor would there ever be again. My pen filled the pages as I journeyed back into the past for the truth, confronting the images branded indelibly on my memory: dressing my baby for the last time; watching the bootee slip from her tiny foot as I handed her to a nurse; my mother waiting patiently with a suitcase in her hand; a nurse scurrying past with a ruched dress and a shawl as another mother asked the unanswerable question: 'Where is your baby?' A plastic wrist tag fading in a drawer.

When I had finished my letter to Sara, I wrote to Michelle. For some reason, perhaps because she was a new mother herself, I needed to explain to her how, after the adoption, I felt I had given up my right ever to be a mother again. I tried to articulate my old anxiety about my daughter turning up on my doorstep one day to find me with a new family. I told her I never wanted to have an unhappy child the wrong side of a happy door.

As the rest of the week unravelled, Michelle called and filled in precious gaps. I learned how, at ten days old, my baby had been given a new life but, strangely, had got to keep a form of her original name since her adoptive parents had always planned to call her Sara. Michelle related how, as a teeneager, Sara had grumbled about not having a middle name and her family had suggested she choose one for herself. Without knowing any of the details of her birth certificate, she had opted for Louise. It was a coincidence, certainly, but having a good friend by that name may have influenced her decision. Perhaps stranger was the fact that Sara had been brought up in Barnes in south-west London. Barnes I couldn't believe it. Throughout the years I'd been living in Wimbledon, my daughter and I had been only three or four miles away from one another.

I keep my appointment with the Post-Adoption Centre and meet a counsellor called Philippa. Warm and sympathetic in reassuring twinset and pearls, she is as taken aback as everyone else by what has happened. Is it possible, she asks, that Sara has engineered this strange 'coincidence'? I think about this. How could she have done so? How could she possibly have taken a job at Hatton & Baker knowing that I would make an appointment it hadn't yet even entered my head to arrange?

I was later to learn that a counsellor at Norcap had suggested to Sara the same explanation in reverse: that perhaps I might have stage-managed our meeting. I knew for certain that I hadn't. And no one else could have offered a remotely plausible theory as to how I might have done so, since I had no means of even finding out my daughter's name, let alone her place of work.

The event was so phenomenal nobody could accept that it might simply have been an astonishing coincidence. Everyone was searching for a more complex explanation. Could it be synchronicity? Fate? Divine intervention? Seeking some kind of scientific answer, I found myself reading up on synchronicity – the significant coming together of two apparently unrelated incidents – and morphic resonance, the theory that memory has a basis in nature and that the mysterious, almost telepathic interconnections seen in organisms can be attributed to a collective memory within species. Have human beings somehow retained the vestiges of whatever it is that drives ants and bees to organise themselves effectively and efficiently within their colonies? Do we give off some kind of signal that other human beings can pick up?

I could be sure of only one thing. I had always been convinced that one day my daughter and I would meet. It was just a matter of when, and maybe up to now the time simply hadn't been right.

Looking back, it seems to me that for perhaps two years or more I had been unconsciously laying the foundations for this meeting, putting in place all the elements of the environment I needed to have ready for that day – home, career, lifestyle, outlook, security – to create a space my daughter could comfortably enter. From the age of thirty-five onwards I had at long last been doing my 'layette'. When I'd studied my reflection in the bathroom mirror that morning before going to

Jermyn Street, maybe I had been acknowledging, for the first time in a more conscious way, that everything was in order. Now was the right moment for us to meet. My layette was complete.

In the week-long hiatus between finding Sara and meeting her, all I could do, it seemed, was cry. My friends worried about me. It was as if all the tears I'd been unable to shed for twenty years had been stored in some great lake and once the dam had burst, the flood was unstoppable.

I spent time with Mark – who had by this time given up music and was working with young homeless people as a counsellor – talking through the concerns and developments that were arising on a daily basis. Someone had offered the suggestion that I didn't have to meet Sara if I didn't feel able to handle it. Mark read my mind. 'I know,' he said. 'How could you possibly *not* meet her?' Not in a million years would I have avoided this encounter, however earth-shattering it might prove to be.

Seb, too, was awestruck by what had happened and had passed on the news to a lot of people on my behalf. Most had been confounded or fascinated but one had actually offered sympathy. 'Poor Julie,' said a mutual acquaintance who chose to look at things from another perspective. She had instantly grasped that, since my daughter had been adopted because of my age and social circumstances, when I met her, I would be meeting a stranger from a middle-class home. 'How will they ever connect?' she had asked Seb despairingly.

I fretted about this potential problem. I thought about poor Pip Pirrip in *Great Expectations*, who discovers that the rough criminal Magwitch is his true benefactor, and not, as he has assumed, the genteel Miss Havisham. I did not want to disappoint my daughter or destroy any illusions she might have about me. But I consoled myself with the knowledge that Dickens uses the character of Magwitch to show that class is an artificial construct. What matters is what lies in our hearts. That is what will connect or divide us.

At last we were ready to arrange a meeting. Where should it take place? Tina kindly offered us the use of her lovely new home in Bayswater but I felt the venue should be on neutral territory, and somewhere both public and private, where Sara and I could talk confidentially without being overheard while maintaining a steadying foothold in the world going on around us. Perhaps somewhere in the open air.

We agree on the Pagoda in Kew Gardens at three o'clock on the Sunday afternoon. Michelle acts as go-between, relaying and confirming the details. I know she is affected by all this. Her voice quavers on the phone during these conversations. Until the beginning of this week she was a complete stranger but now we are like two sisters caught up in a family drama. She has been the catalyst for this reunion and I thank her for everything she has done. She responds, warmly, that she hopes all will go well. Before ringing off, she remembers something.

'By the way, I don't think I've mentioned it, but Sara has short, blonde hair.' And then she is gone.

I put down the receiver, trying to absorb the implications of what she's just said. My own hair is long and dark. Martin's was a mousy mid-brown in the years we were together. Is it common for brown- and dark-haired parents to have a blonde child? Might Martin have been fair as a small boy? I don't know. In any case, Sara is grown up now. I'm gripped by a sudden fear.

Could there possibly have been a mistake?

Three o'clock at the Pagoda. At five o'clock in the morning my bedroom looks as though it has been ransacked by burglars. I have tried on every piece of clothing I own but still I don't know what to wear. I have decided against high heels, but all of my footwear seems frivolous. Eventually I unearth a pair of sensible black boots. Now, hours later, I am putting them on for the third time with a pair of sensible black trousers. They peek out sensibly from beneath the hems. I am also wearing a black rollneck sweater and have tied my long hair back from my face. I check myself in the mirror. I look like a policewoman. Juliet Bravo. I reach for a dusky pink checked jacket chosen, after a great deal of deliberation, a while earlier. I put on a slick of lipstick and then wipe it off again.

Finally I leave the house.

I am determined to arrive early. If there is one thing in my life for which I must not be late, it is surely this

– a date with my daughter. Elephant and Castle tube station is comparatively quiet as today is a Sunday. It is 11 November. Remembrance Sunday. I descend in a lift to the dusty platform, board the train that arrives in a rush of wind, change on to the District Line for Kew. Might I have been quicker taking the overground from Waterloo? It doesn't matter. I emerge from Kew station with plenty of time to spare. But then I enter the gardens through the wrong entrance. Now I am faced with a long walk, past the glass walls and domed roof of the Palm House, beyond the scented Rose Garden and past pockets of milling tourists.

A view I encounter suddenly overlaps with an image in my memory. I am disconcerted for a moment and then I place it: the pictures I had pasted into photograph albums with my mother as a child. My dad, laughing, chasing a baby as she crawls across a lawn. A toddler standing under a tree, wrapped up against the chill of a winter's day, like this one. My parents, Sara's grandparents, used to bring me here. Perhaps, at this very moment, I am treading the same ground we once walked across together.

'She has short, blonde hair…' A blonde woman passes me and my heart swells.

Could this be her? She turns slightly to one side as she walks on and I can see that she is at least fifty years old. My body is responding to triggers over which I have no control, like the body of a new mother, which is, in a way, what I am.

I walk on and at last the Pagoda is rising in front of me, all 160 feet of it. An impressive piece of eighteenth-century Chinoiserie, it's a memorable landmark for such a significant meeting. The kind of location Hitchcock might have chosen for the final scene of a movie. Is this an ending? Or a beginning?

I sit down on a park bench beneath the Pagoda to wait, looking out on to a green lawn, trees and the various paths that all lead to this point.

'Poor Julie.' Perhaps my friend is right. Perhaps my daughter only wants to meet me to satisfy some curiosity. One brief encounter and she might go her own way, back to her life and her family. She has had a good upbringing in a big house in Barnes. What does she have in common with me, a child with no bedroom who lunched daily on pie, mash and liquor?

We may be strangers but we are bound by blood, by history and by those brief summer days we spent together when I whispered secrets into the gateway to her mind. Perhaps she might not even come—

I catch sight of someone. No, two people. A woman in her forties walking with a young woman, approaching at a distance along a path to the left of me.

The girl has short, blonde hair.

Clothes not unlike my own. Black jacket, trousers, boots.

They have almost reached me, but the girl veers suddenly away from the Pagoda. She is walking on… Then, as though summoning her courage, she turns back. She is moving towards me.

I see her now, straight in front of me: my own grown-up baby, smiling back at me, my face in hers.

Somehow I have got to my feet. My body knows what to do even if my brain doesn't. What am I going to say? What words could come close to bridging the separation of all these years? I take a few steps forwards, relying on my body. I trust my body now, as it seems to be the only part of me that is functioning. It is aching to hold her.

'Can I give you a hug?' My voice is a hoarse whisper but suddenly she is there in my arms. We cling to one another tightly. I taste in one salt kiss our tears mingled together on her cheek. The world has shifted on its axis. Nothing will ever be the same. 'You have my face,' I say, as though she might have stolen it.

The woman I had noticed stands in the shadows. A family friend has accompanied Sara. My daughter asks the woman to leave us for a moment and we move to the shelter of the Pagoda. Sitting on a bench, we nervously take cigarette packs from our pockets and hold lighter flames for each other. We draw deep, smoky breaths. Our hands dance through the air as we speak, legs crossed at the same angle as though, in spite of all the years we have been separated – our genes and souls still know we are one, have maybe even engineered our reunion.

Sara has read my letter and it's time for questions. We begin to fill in the blank spaces of our lives. As she speaks I realise how near we must have been to one another over the years. As well as growing up in Barnes while I was in Wimbledon, she has spent a lot of time in Spain, where her family lived for a while. Many, many times in our lives perhaps we have been separated by only a few miles.

The family friend walks at a distance, keeping a protective eye on her charge. She was once Sara's ballet teacher, I am told. I learn that Sara was a good dancer, that she had a chance to work with the Joffrey in New York. I remember black plimsolls bound with ribbon, tiptoeing across the creaky floorboards at Lefevre Road. A Dying Swan.

'How did you feel?' I ask. 'When you saw my name on the script?'

She lowers her eyes and shakes her head slightly, as though she's seeing it all over again. 'I couldn't believe it,' she replies softly. 'Michelle took one look at me and knew something was wrong. I was shaking. The words just tumbled out. "That's the name of my mother."'

She gazes back at me now, as though to make sure I'm here, that this isn't a dream.

'She must've thought I was mad. She said that you'd been in the office just the day before, that I'd brought you both coffee. She insisted she must have introduced us – she always introduces secretaries to clients – and maybe she did, but she couldn't have mentioned your surname or the coffee would've ended up in your lap.'

We both laugh, suddenly, nervously, relieved we share a sense of humour. The tension eases. I see the family friend relaxing too as she circles at a distance.

Sara continues: 'I tried really hard to remember seeing you in the office.'

'Me too,' I whisper.

'Michelle thought I was mistaken. She said you were too young. But I knew it had to be you. It's a strange name, isn't it?'

I smile and thank God for my strange name.

'I told her to ring you,' she continues. 'Straight away. I told her she must. I had to know for sure.'

I remember the call coming through in my busy office. Had it really only been on Tuesday? The tone of Michelle's voice. Something was wrong. She had something to tell me, she said. How could I ever have possibly guessed it could be this? Whatever I told her could stay within her office walls. But all the while, Sara had been on the other side of the door, waiting for her answer.

Tell her it's me.

'She came out of her office and just looked at me,' Sara goes on. 'She had tears in her eyes and she said, "Sara, we've just found your mother."'

Sara looks confident but her body gives her away. She has my mother's nervous hand, its tremor satisfied by a cigarette. I reach into my bag and take from it photographs, ghosts from the past: Margaret Mary Exley and Bill Wassmer, and Martin, her father. She stares down at the missing pieces of her life.

'I always knew you were there,' she says.

'I always knew you would find me,' I reply.

She tells me about seeing her birth certificate for the first time. Names on a page. Occupations: 'Spinster' and 'demolition worker'. No illusions, no chance to indulge in teenage flights of fancy about having royal blood.

'When I saw your names there in black and white, suddenly, you became real people.'

She had tried to seek us out but, with my mother's maisonette handed back to the council and all trace of the Wassmers erased, had come up against a brick wall at Gullane House. It had been the same story with Martin and Bridie.

'I just felt probably the time wasn't right.'

I look down at my hand, at the two rings I'd taken from my mother's hand in St Thomas' Hospital: her wedding ring and my Irish grandmother's single gold band. I slip from my finger the one that belonged to the grandmother I never met and give it to Sara – a link with her past. And it fits. She sits close beside me, twenty years old, no longer imagined but real. I take in every facet, every inch of her, as she talks on. All too soon the family friend arrives, a signal that our meeting is at an end.

Is this an ending? Or a beginning?

I take a deep breath. 'Would you like to meet again?'

My grown-up daughter pauses. Then she smiles.

Chapter Fifteen

Emotional Journeys

The day after our meeting in Kew Gardens, Sara wrote me a letter.

Dear Julie,

I just felt like writing to you to say thank you. What for? I'm not totally sure! But our meeting on Sunday was perhaps one of the best things that has ever happened to me.

I had the urge to write to you and now I've started I'm not quite sure what I want to say! I am glad that things have worked so well and although I have no demands of you, I hope and feel that as time goes on we can build a relationship as friends. I want to thank you for the ring you gave me. Whatever happens I will treasure it always.

There is still so much I want to learn from you and about you and I hope you don't think I'm being 'pushy'!

I hope you don't mind me writing this letter, I just felt the urge to do so. I will ring this week.

All my love, Sara xx

As I reached the final line, I smiled. My tears were all dried up, as though a period of mourning had ended. In the days that followed I read the letter over and over again, studying the handwriting – big, bold letters, not unlike my own.

A week later, I travelled up to Jermyn Street again, not to see Michelle this time, but my daughter. My daughter. I heard myself saying this constantly, just to relish the feel of the words in my mouth. Two words that, in combination, I had barely allowed myself to utter in twenty years.

We were going out to lunch. I arrived at the offices of Hatton & Baker to find Sara on the phone. Michelle was off for the day and another secretary offered me a seat in Sara's office. Everyone who worked there had heard about what had happened. Now they sneaked glances at me as I waited for Sara to finish her business call. She put down the receiver and looked across at me without speaking.

'Are you OK?' I asked tentatively.

'Fine,' she smiled. We greeted one another with a kiss, she grabbed her jacket and we set off together for a little Italian restaurant round the corner. As we walked towards Piccadilly, I noticed how the white jeans she was wearing emphasised her long, rangy legs. Martin's legs.

At the restaurant, we were shown to a table and handed menus. More interested in studying each other, we scarcely glanced at them. It felt, oddly, like being on a date. We were both curious about one another and full of wonder at what had happened to us, agreeing that it felt a little like falling in love. I invited Sara to choose whatever she would like from the menu, suddenly aware that I was sounding like a frequently absent parent trying to make up with a treat for the lack of attention paid to a child. How on earth could I ever compensate for twenty years' absence from Sara's life? It dawned on me then that I hadn't the faintest idea of my daughter's tastes in food, or in anything else, come to that.

I was thrown off balance for a moment. There was no plot, no script for this relationship. No correct etiquette, even. But a glass of wine broke the ice. Soon we were chatting away animatedly like old friends. Or was it new friends? It was hard to classify our feelings at this point. Each meeting stirred up strong emotions and yet we didn't know each other. We were on a journey to one another.

When I offered a polite '*grazie*' to the Italian waiter who took our order, Sara asked if I spoke Italian. I told her that, as a result of my adventures aboard the *Golden Sunset*, my Spanish was better.

'I speak a bit of Spanish too,' she said. She had told me by the Pagoda that she had spent time in Spain. I wondered whether this was where she had been taken on the holiday for which my consent had been requested before the adoption papers were signed. But I didn't ask that now. Instead, I just watched her as she talked, fascinated by every feature, still not quite able to comprehend that this was my living, breathing, grown-up girl.

In every gesture, every intonation she is familiar to me. She is buoyed up by my father's confidence. She blinks with Martin's long eyelashes and my mother's smile creeps across her face. My own voice speaks to me but the eyes are Bridie's – big and blue. Poor Bridie. I think of her sadness on the day I went into hospital; how she had wept at the thought that she would never know her first grandchild. And yet, by some miracle, two decades later, that grandchild is here, chatting away to me across a table in a cheerful trattoria. My daughter is the sum of so many people and yet she is a different person. Her own person. Sara.

We strolled back to the office, saying not goodbye, but *arriverderci*!

A thank-you card soon arrived in the post. Inside the envelope were photographs, two of Sara as a teenager and one of her as a little girl, standing in a sunny garden. It was the garden I had always imagined. From the picture, my daughter looks out at me across the years, head turned to one side, a coy smile for the camera, her long hair tied up in a platinum blonde ponytail. This is the photograph I had waited for all this time. Now Sara had given it to me herself.

I proudly showed the snapshots to friends, acquaintances, anyone who demonstrated the slightest interest.

I would soon be leaving Sara for a while. Tina was to be married in Jamaica and had very generously bought me an air ticket so that I could be at the wedding. We were all to spend nearly a fortnight on the island, so the next few days were filled with frenzied activity both at work and at home. I hired an outfit for the occasion, packed a suitcase and made the time to write another letter, this one to Sara's mum. I knew how hard the situation must be for her and I hoped that if I sent it now, shortly before leaving the country, by the time she received my letter, the knowledge that I was thousands of miles away might give her some space in which to read it and decide how, or whether, to reply, without feeling under any pressure to do either.

It was a hard letter to write, not least because my daughter's mother was a stranger to me. I fully acknowledged that Sara was, and always would be, her daughter. I wrote that I knew she must be proud of her, and that she should be proud of herself, too, for bringing her up so well. I understood if she wanted to keep her distance. The reason I was writing was simply to thank her, to recognise a connection that would always be between us and to ask if, when I returned, she would like to meet, if only for a quick cup of tea. I phrased my letter carefully. I didn't want her to feel I was invading her world, just that I was holding out my hand to her. If she preferred not to take it, that was fine.

A week later I was in St Mary's Bay, Jamaica. Tina and her husband-to-be, both perfectionists, had planned a huge itinerary of fabulous activities for their guests. We rafted the Rio Grande, slid down the Dunn's River Falls and wandered through the rooms of Noël Coward's house, Firefly. The wedding itself, held in the grounds of a fifteenth-century-style Venetian villa with gardens full of hibiscus, was simply magical, more like a movie set than anything I had known in real life. I thought of the romantic films I had seen so many times with my mother, of Katharine Hepburn and Cary Grant, Clark Gable and Carole Lombard. If only my mum could have seen me now. When she was alive I had always brought back holiday souvenirs for her and entertained her with tales of my adventures. I could buy nothing for her now but I could take something home for Sara. In a bustling Jamaican market I came across a trinket box topped with a small painting by a local artist. Perfect.

On the flight home I thought about the other person caught up in our emotional triangle and wondered how my letter had been received. Back in the tiny flat on Merrow Street, I sifted through the mail on my doormat. There was no reply from Sara's mother.

I understood completely. I knew what it was like to experience two worlds colliding.

Once I'd settled back into my London routine, I invited Sara to a party, an industry ball hosted by the Guild of Film Stuntmen. I took her to Debbie's flat in Notting Hill, where she met Debbie, Jools and Tina and we got ready for the do, all girls together, sipping wine as we slipped into party clothes in front of a bedroom mirror. Separated as we were by only seventeen years, in many ways we were now behaving more like long-lost sisters than mother and daughter. As we stood side by side, checking our outfits in a bedroom mirror, the other girls gathered round us and studied our reflections. We looked like twins, they said, one dark and one fair, like photographic positives and negatives. Sara borrowed my make-up and called me Julie. Another woman was Mum, and always would be: the woman who had nursed her through measles and chicken pox and put up with outbreaks of teenage rebellion. I wondered whether they had been as bad as mine. Had my daughter pelted student teachers with wet clay as soon as their backs were turned? All I knew at that stage was that Sara had studied for a B. Tech Business Diploma and was keen to become an actors' agent. At her age, I'd been certain of nothing except what I didn't want.

As we set off for the party, Sara linked her arm in mine. We were finding our way, inch by inch, towards a comfortable place in each other's hearts. Two hours later, music was playing and I was dancing with my daughter. Flashbulbs popped all around us. New photographs to cherish.

Only weeks after Sara and I had found one another, the offices of Hatton & Baker were disbanded. The partners were going their separate ways, Michelle to start up her own agency representing writers and directors. I realised that if I had left it even a short while longer to approach Michelle and make an appointment to see her, my daughter would never have been in place to read my name upon a script. How narrow the window of opportunity had been! I had been fully occupied by the gargantuan challenge of making my housing association flat fit to live in and could so easily have put it off. But something had been driving me on to draw together all the threads of my life, in preparation for this moment. Truly, it had been the right time.

Sara left Jermyn Street, too. Her boss asked if she would like to carry on working for him in an office at his home. It transpired that he lived in Camberwell, just five minutes in the car from my flat in Merrow Street. It was a measure of our growing familiarity that when she visited me now for supper, I knew what she liked to eat. Sometimes she would stay over rather than risk a late-night journey home, and in the mornings I'd make tea for her, pausing, cup in hand, to steal a glimpse of her as she lay sleeping in the living room. Could this beautiful girl really be the same tiny child who had slept beside me in a hospital cot, the same baby I had placed in another woman's arms? The years had made a woman of Sara, too, but, amazingly, she was back with me once more, curled up on my sofa bed.

On 3 June 1991, three women sat at a table in London's Ivy restaurant. All around us, serious-looking men were talking business, but the mood on our table was celebratory. It was Sara's twenty-first birthday. I had brought with me a large fabric bag stuffed with individually wrapped gifts. As Sara opened them excitedly, Michelle caught my eye. She knew I was still trying vainly to compensate for the past, but she simply smiled and called me Mary Poppins. She was, after all, part of this miracle, a fairy godmother to our reunion, and this was a day for rejoicing in it. We raised our glasses for a toast. Surely life couldn't get any better?

The fairytale quality of those days was soon to be brought to an end. Within the next three years I would lose my two oldest friends to terminal illnesses. First it was Mark, my soulmate over some seventeen years. As his condition deteriorated I spent as much time with him as I could but when he died a year later, in August 1992, the shock was still immense and I was inconsolable. By this stage, Seb was also beginning to suffer worrying health problems. I could not understand how, having been blessed by fortunate coincidence so often in recent years, I was now confronting a double tragedy. I was completely winded by all the emotional extremes I had experienced in such a short period

I had discovered after Mark died that he had left me some money from an insurance policy in his will. It was a large sum, more than I had ever seen in my whole life, but I felt bad about accepting it, as if I were somehow profiting from his death. It was a time of great upheaval, with gains overshadowed by terrible loss.

One day, I found myself crying in my car on the way to work. Once I had started, I was unable to stop.

I needed help to get through this and I embarked upon several weeks of counselling. When it was over, friends convinced me to honour Mark's gift. I decided to use the money to buy his Peckham flat from his estate. I was advised that the best way of handling this was for the property to be offset against the sum he had left me and transferred directly to me from the estate. So I never actually took possession of all that money – but I certainly reaped its rewards.

Tina, Jools and Debbie had put the Knowledge Production Company up for sale and we had produced the last edition of the directory that autumn, so I had been gearing myself up to looking for another full-time job. By enabling me to live rent-free, Mark's bequest liberated me from the nine-to-five treadmill and handed me the opportunity to try to make a living from writing. Now that I had the luxury of time, I could finish projects I had started and build up a body of work. It was the best gift my dear friend could have given me.

I planned to move into Mark's flat, a spacious upper-floor conversion in a Regency-style house in Glengall Road, Peckham, in the New Year of 1993. Sara was in sentimental mood as I packed away my final bits and pieces at Merrow Street.

'It's like the end of an era,' she said, 'This is the place where we got to know one another.'

The sofa bed she had slept on had been given to someone in greater need of it and my little car was stacked to the gills with everything I owned. Late one January evening, I left Merrow Street for the last time, drove the car, suspension almost scraping the tarmac, to Glengall Road and let myself into Mark's flat.

His things were still there, all around me: paintings and prints on the walls, photographs in frames. A pen lay on the table and a jacket hung on the back of a chair as if at any moment he might step into the room and carry on with his life. But he wasn't going to do that; instead, I was taking over the space he had left behind. I poured myself a drink and sat down on the sofa. So many times we had sat here together but now there was only me. I caught sight of my reflection, thrown back at me by the darkening glass of the bare windows across the room. I was resting one arm against the sofa, right knee bent, right ankle on my left knee. This wasn't how I sat. It was how Mark always used to sit.

The realisation brought me up short. I remembered the time, soon after my father's death, when I had sprawled on the sofa in the way he always did, throwing my shoes into the same corner of the room. I tried to make sense of this. Does the absence of those we love become so unbearable that we are compelled to try to take their place? Or is it that, in fleeting moments and in some unfathomable way, the dead may sometimes inhabit us, guiding us from within? That evening I allowed myself to imagine that, although my parents had been lost to me at such a young age, they might yet have been able to influence me in a way they never could while they were alive. Perhaps they had steered me towards Sara – or her towards me. Perhaps Mark, too, might yet guide me in some new direction.

That year, I settled down to focus on my writing and was at long last able to produce a collection of scripts that Michelle could show to film and television companies as examples of my work. When the bank account needed a boost I would take on other assignments – I did some video casting with Debbie and had a job briefly with a film producer – but my principal workplace was my desk at Glengall Road. For the first time in my life I had a garden, too, shared with my downstairs neighbours, young guys who spent a lot of time clubbing so were largely nocturnal. With some help from Mark's mum and dad, I threw myself into taking care of it.

One day Michelle called me to give me some good news. She had arranged for me to meet someone who was looking for new writers for a television drama series.

'Which one?' I asked.

'*EastEnders.*'

Good news indeed. I had never been much interested in television soaps, but *EastEnders* was the exception to the rule – I'd become hooked on it after my return to London in 1988. Within the fictional Albert Square I found elements that resonated with my childhood: bold, engaging characters who struggled with economic or family problems in a world bordered by a pub, a launderette and a bustling street market. Critics sometimes complained that storylines were 'depressing', but to me this was drama dealing with life as it is, not how we'd like it to be. This was definitely my kind of show.

The producer I was to see at the BBC Elstree studios was Jane Fallon, now better known as a successful novelist and the partner of Ricky Gervais. Coincidentally, she had once worked at Hatton & Baker.

At the studio gates I was handed an identity badge and asked to sign my name in a visitors' book. Jane had arranged to meet me in the canteen and I headed straight there, catching sight, en route, of faces so familiar I almost said hello to them – until I realised they belonged to Walford's Ian Beale and Pauline Fowler.

Sitting down with a cup of tea, I spotted Pat Butcher's son, the recalcitrant David Wicks, at the salad counter. I even offered him a smile as he passed me: if I never got to work on this show, at least I had made contact with one of my favourite characters.

When Jane arrived she told me she had enjoyed reading the scripts Michelle had sent her and wanted to start me on a 'shadow' scheme. This would involve writing a dummy *EastEnders* episode and working on subsequent drafts with an editor, just as I would if it were going to be transmitted. In reality, however, I would be 'shadowing' another writer, who would be producing the real script. I discovered that the guy I would be shadowing was someone I had met on the residential writers' course I'd attended in Devon.

I left the studios with a head full of ideas, a bagful of information on the history of the programme and its characters and a sheaf of scripts to digest. The first-ever episode, broadcast in 1985, had opened with Arthur Fowler, Den Watts and Ali Osman breaking down a door to find an elderly neighbour close to death in a stinking sitting room. Reg Cox hadn't been seen by his neighbours for the past three days. Now, as they watched him being taken off to hospital, the residents of Albert Square revealed themselves in a dialogue about the nature of community that dovetailed, realistically and entertainingly, with everyday conversations about pregnancy and pease pudding. I loved every line, but I was daunted by the prospect of writing such scenes myself.

A week or so later, however, I had managed to complete my shadow episode. My editor made only a few tweaks and the writer of the real episode joked that she should transmit mine instead, save him a job and he and I could share his fee. Suddenly I was writing my own episodes for transmission and working regularly on what would become Britain's most popular soap.

When I joined the show, it was going out only twice a week and I was one of around thirty drama writers contributing either one or both of the week's episodes. We attended regular meetings at which, fuelled by endless cups of coffee and cigarettes, we decided the fates of well-loved characters or despised villains. At that time, it could take up to three months to complete a single episode for filming. Several drafts would be required, often to accommodate new story developments, cast illness or general continuity problems between programmes.

The first episode I wrote for transmission concerned the tensions between a young Michelle and the rest of the Fowler family as she strove to bring up her illegitimate daughter. I sensed that writing for this show would prove cathartic, and so it proved. I drew inspiration from my childhood for eccentric characters like Dot Cotton and Jack Branning, who were not so far removed from Aunt Carrie and Uncle Will, and used my own emotional experience to judge the complex reactions of David Wicks on discovering that he was the natural father of Bianca Jackson. When Bianca's younger sister, Sonia, gave birth to a baby girl who was subsequently adopted, I had no need to call upon my imagination.

While working on these episodes, I did some research on current attitudes to adoption. Nowadays, if birth parents wanted their child to be able to contact them once he or she had reached eighteen, they had the right to register that wish with an intermediary agency, such as a local authority or adoption agency. Detailed information about the birth family and the baby would in any case be kept on file for the child to access later. Apart from anything else, it was important for adopted children to be able to find out about any medical history that might affect them, such as inherited illnesses.

The emotional and psychological impact of adoption had been recognised and was better understood, too. Increasingly, secrecy was being viewed as unhealthy. Parents were now actively encouraged to provide diaries and albums containing photographs, documents and letters to accompany their children to their new homes. These could be used by adoptive parents to help explain to children where they came from or saved so that the child could learn about his history at a later date.

In one episode of this *EastEnders* storyline, I decided that Sonia would compile an album like this for her lost child, including photographs and stories and information about her family, so that baby Chloe would never have to wonder about her roots or question whether she had been loved by her mother.

Writing such scenes seemed to make up in some small way for what I had been unable to do for Sara. Chloe would have her family album while for my own daughter, two names on a birth certificate and some baby clothes had had to suffice. I began to recognise why, on a hot summer's day in a corridor of the Mother's Hospital, the sight of a nurse hurrying away with a ruched dress and a shawl had unleashed the pent-up sorrow I had tried so hard to contain. I had grieved that day, not just for myself, but for my baby girl, understanding viscerally that these few pitiful items, bought from a market with saved pocket money, were the only evidence she would ever have that I loved her. If she were never to receive them, how could she ever know that?

Even the scant official record of our relationship hadn't been enough for Sara to find me. It had taken my script to do that. Michelle always said she felt I had been constantly struggling to lead another life; to escape the confines of the East End and my family expectations. Writing was a big part of that and it was writing, ultimately, that had led me back to my daughter. Funnily enough, in a way I couldn't possibly have predicted, it had also brought me back to the East End – professionally, if not physically.

When an envelope dropped through my door containing an invitation to an *EastEnders* anniversary party in London, I didn't need to think too hard about who to take as my 'plus one'. Sara and I travelled by cab from Glengall Road to Kensington High Street, drawing up outside the art-deco façade of the old Derry & Toms building that had, for a few brief, heady years in the early 1970s, been home to the famous Biba store.

A doorman took our invitations and directed us past the jostling paparazzi eager to snap members of the cast. I remembered how I had once wandered the lower floors of this building, a troubled teenager searching for a new identity among the Biba clothes and smoky eye shadows. Now I was stepping out of a lift on to its roof, my daughter beside me, and we were being guided towards the acre and a half of palms and exotic greenery that made up Kensington Roof Gardens, the largest roof gardens in Europe. A waiter offered us glasses of champagne. This was no soap opera – this was for real.

I was later to write for other drama shows, too. In Manchester I worked on a Granada hospital series called *Medics*, starring Jimmi Harkishin (now Dev in *Coronation Street*), former Dr Who Tom Baker and Sue Johnston from *The Royle Family* and *Waking the Dead*. I also wrote for the LWT series *London's Burning*, based on an original TV drama by Jack Rosenthal. A big budget gave writers the chance to go to town with spectacular disasters requiring expensive special effects, which was very liberating for someone accustomed to writing scenes for characters who spent most of their lives in hospital wards or pubs. I was still working on original projects, too. The wolf was a long way from my door and I reminded myself on almost a daily basis that I had Mark to thank for that, offering him a silent message of gratitude from my heart.

Seb had been pleased when I started writing for *EastEnders.* He tried to catch all my episodes and pumped me for stories about the production and cast. By the end of 1993, however, his illness was taking hold and that Christmas, I wasn't in the mood for celebrating.

I felt that doing something useful with people who had more sadness in their lives than I had might put things in perspective, so I rang up the Elephant and Castle branch of the Salvation Army and asked if they needed any help over the festive season. Since giving birth to Sara at the Salvation Army Mothers' Hospital, I'd always felt an affinity with Salvationists and often put money in their collecting tins. I was grateful for the kindness I had been shown at the hospital and admired the officers for the quiet way they demonstrated their faith through action.

I ended up helping to cook Christmas lunch for a crowd of mainly homeless and elderly guests and brought with me small stocking-filler presents wrapped in multiple layers of paper for a game of pass-the-parcel. Most of the officers helping out seemed very shy. When the time came for a visit from Santa nobody wanted the role so they asked me to do it. The outfit was somewhat on the baggy side, reminding me of the hideous orange red devil costume I had tried on all those years ago in the pursuit of 'easy money'. I smiled, missing the way Mark would have been reacting as I adjusted Santa's white moustache-and-beard combo. A mother and now Mother Christmas: who'd have thought it?

My star possibly waned a little when it came to pass-the-parcel, however. The music stopped while the parcel was in the hands of a Salvation Army sergeant. He removed a layer of paper and promptly blushed furiously. I'd used old newspapers and magazines to wrap the package and he had revealed a glossy colour photograph of a man posing in his underpants, muscles rippling. It was only an ad for aftershave, but from the look on the sergeant's face you'd have thought I'd exposed him to a page from *Hustler*.

Having got through Christmas I visited Seb, who was entertained by the story of my Salvation Army festivities. He was not in good shape. I had hoped to be looking forward to a brighter year in 1994 but before long my dear friend was seriously ill and by August he was dead. Again my world was turned upside down.

Chapter Sixteen

Full Circle

Several months after Seb's death a memorial gathering was held at the Royal Geographical Society in Kensington. He'd had so many friends, and most of them were here. The first person I saw on arriving was the singer Kirsty MacColl, who I'd got to know when Seb made the pop promo for her single 'New England'. We chatted, recalling an evening on which the three of us had sat together in the recording studio of Kirsty's Ealing home, drinking wine and listening to her new album, *Kite*. One track on it had stayed with me, a Ray Davies song called 'Days' – a simple, beautiful melody that Kirsty had sung so effortlessly in her distinctive folksy voice. The lyrics seemed especially poignant now.

...I bless the light
I bless the light that lights on you, believe me,
And though you're gone,
You're with me every single day, believe me.

Kirsty had heard on the grapevine about how I had found my daughter but didn't know I was now writing for TV. She was intrigued by all the changes in my life and invited me to come for lunch some time soon with her brother Hamish and her children.

As we talked my eyes were drawn to a man standing nearby. He was wearing a familiar leather jacket. Suddenly he turned, as though he had become aware that I was watching him. Tall, dark, caramel-coloured eyes... I recognised him now from photographs I had seen in Seb's albums. In fact, I had even met him once, very briefly, at a birthday party. 'Kas' Kasparian.

'I know that jacket,' I said to him.

Kas glanced reflexively down at it. 'Seb gave it to me. It came with the badges so I left them on.' Two tiny buttons were still pinned to the lapel, one promoting the dance group Kissing the Pink, the other the reggae artist Gregory Isaacs – small but aching reminders of our lost friend.

I learned that Kas had flown over from Los Angeles for the memorial. Although he had been living in California for the past twenty years, he had remained in touch with many old friends from Notting Hill, friends we had in common like Adam, the builder who had been living at the Westy when I first moved in.

Adam was here, too, having flown over from France, but, before I had a chance to speak to him properly, the memorial was over and we were all spilling out on to the dark street, lost and somewhat bewildered, until somebody suggested it seemed only fitting that we should repair, as we had always done to round off an evening, to the Westy for 'one last drink'.

An hour or so later, I found myself looking around the living room of my former home at a mix of Seb's Bohemian friends talking, drinking, crying or dancing to his old records, which were playing on without him on his stereo. I had lost track of Kas but then the doorbell rang and he was back again, unwrapping steaming paper on the table to reveal mountains of warm fish and chips.

'I thought people might be hungry,' he smiled.

The party continued on for a while but without our beloved host it was losing momentum and I was soon outside on Ledbury Road, waiting to hail a cab to take me home, for the very last time, from the Westy. Others were trickling out of the front door having decided to go on to an Indian restaurant. It was difficult for anyone to say goodbye. I knew Adam would be flying back to his wife and children in Toulouse the following evening so I asked if he would like to come over to Glengall Road the next day for Sunday lunch before he left. He said he'd love to.

Back at the flat, a thought that was niggling me prompted me to dig out the old address book I'd used when I first went sailing. Its cover was battered, held in place by an elastic band, the pages bleached by sunlight and splashes of salt water. Flicking through it, I found what I was after. I was right. Years ago, the Captain had scribbled down a name and telephone number in this book for someone he thought he might look up if ever he took the boat to California. The name was there in the Captain's fading handwriting. Kas Kasparian.

The next day, Adam arrived for lunch, slightly late, apologetic, and with a surprise guest in tow. It was Kas Kasparian again. This time on my doorstep.

At that stage I didn't possess a proper oven in which to cook a Sunday roast, so I went Italian and made a spaghetti dish. We spent a relaxed afternoon together, chatting and reminiscing, but there was an undercurrent to our conversation. The shock of Seb's untimely death was causing us all to take stock of our lives.

I discovered that Kas had visited London while I was sailing and had been accommodated for a few days by Seb in my unoccupied room at the Westy. He admitted now that he had looked around at all my photographs and books on the shelves, which had made him curious about me. I learned that his grown-up son, Gabriel, worked with him in the States but that his teenage daughter, Moon, lived here in London with her mother. She visited Kas in America but work prevented him from spending very long in London.

The only way he could see more of her was to move back to England.

Adam pressed me to tell my own story, the extra-ordinary tale of how Sara had re-entered my life. Sitting in Mark's flat that day, I was conscious of how many connections there seemed to be between us all – Mark, Seb, Adam, the Captain, Kas and me – so many strands running through our lives, sometimes crossing, some-times interweaving, sometimes looping off for a while. Now they were all being gathered together in the vivid memories we shared of the two friends we had lost.

Kas had only one more day in London before his flight back to the States but he returned the following evening to say thank you for lunch by taking me for supper. He arrived on my doorstep bearing flowers, and we decided to go for a walk, calling in at the bustling Pizzeria Castello on the Walworth Road for two quat-tro formaggi pizzas to take with us to eat on the Thames Embankment. At Cleopatra's Needle, he confided that although he had just finished building a large house for himself in Los Angeles, he felt, in some ways, rootless.

Kas had been born in Nicosia in 1945 to Armenian parents, but the family had fled Cyprus for Devon in England in 1956, worried about the escalating conflict over independence that would indeed go on to result in civil war. The Kasparians had finally settled in Ealing, where Kas had completed his schooling. Like the guy in the old Dusty Springfield song, he was 'the son of a preacher man'; like me he was a rebel, too, and had chosen an alternative path. As Jack Kerouac and Hunter S. Thompson had done before him, in the late 1960s, he headed off on the hippy trail to California, ending up at Big Sur.

As we sat together on a bench overlooking the river I imagined what an amazing time this must have been. Eight years younger than Kas, I would still have been at school, getting only as far as Tottenham Court Road to buy hippy bells to wear around my neck, while Kas was doing the real thing: travelling to California to be right at the beating heart of the 'peace and love' movement.

He told me how he had lived in a cabin perched high above the Pacific Ocean on land belonging to the photographer and explorer Giles Healey, one of the first non-Mayans to lay eyes on the Bonampak temples in Chiapas, Mexico, where he had been taken in 1946 by local tribesmen to see one of the ancient murals. Healey owned 150 acres on Partington Ridge on Big Sur and had himself once lived in this cabin, which he'd bought for 'the price of a small refrigerator'. Now he allowed Kas to have it rent-free in return for taking care of the land and the house he now occupied with his artist wife Sheila and their family.

This was a community that had long welcomed free thinkers. The writer Henry Miller had said of his own discovery of Big Sur in 1947: 'It was the beginning of something more than a friendship. It was an initiation into a new way of life.' When Kas had arrived twenty-odd years later, he felt exactly the same way. He would work on the upkeep of Giles's land during the day and in the evenings drive down the Pacific Coast highway to the Nepenthe bar, where local writers and artists would congregate (and where Henry Miller himself had played ping-pong).

A few years later Kas settled into his own home on Point Dume. One afternoon, having just picked up his son from school and parked up his car, he noticed a man walking over to him, wearing a red bandana and a donkey jacket with the sleeves cut off. As the man tapped on Kas's car window Gabriel recognised him as the father of one of his schoolfriends. Kas recognised him, too. He wound down his window.

'Nice car,' the man said, running his eyes over Kas's red 1953 Buick convertible. 'Care to sell it?'

'I only just got it,' Kas replied.

'Well, man, if you ever change your mind, I live on Point Dume and my name's Bob.'

'I know,' said Kas. He had recognised the man as Bob Dylan.

I smiled at this, remembering a boy I had once loved, many years before, who had worn his hair just like Dylan wore his on the cover of the *Blonde on Blonde* album.

Ten years later Kas was living in Malibu, where he set up a successful design and construction company, but clearly money was far from being his god: in the

1980s he'd made several trips to Nicaragua as part of a voluntary organisation building houses for people displaced by the conflict between the populist Sandinista government and the US-funded Contras. As he talked of his experiences I saw that, in many ways, Kas's religion was, like my father's, political consciousness. I was beginning to regret that he would be returning to Los Angeles the next morning.

As soon as Kas arrived back in LA, however, I had a phone call from him.

'I'm coming back to London to visit you.'

'When?'

'Next weekend!'

Kas was as good as his word. In fact he returned for three weekends in succession, spending a small fortune on air fares and suffering appalling jet lag. Everyone said it had to be love. Sara was introduced to Kas in the course of these visits. There were drinks evenings and dinner parties at the flat, or we'd all go to a Greek restaurant to eat dolmas and moussaka and listen to Kas's tales of growing up in Cyprus. Sara was charmed. 'I approve!' she beamed. The nature of the unique relationship between Sara and me tended to shift according to the situation: sometimes we were like sisters, other times best friends, often the daughter and mother we actually were. In these weeks, with me caught up in excitement and romance like a besotted teenager, it was as if Sara were the mother and I were the daughter.

She was convinced that it was only a matter of time before Kas would propose. She was spot on. At the end of his third weekend in London, he popped the question. 'Shall we get married?' How would I respond? I was forty-two years old and had lived an independent life for years. This had all happened so quickly and, with the distance between us, so far it had all been a bit like an ongoing holiday romance. Had I finally met the right man? Or was it that the right man had finally come along once everything was else was in place?

Before long Kas had sold his house in the States, moved back to London permanently and, having already fallen in love, we had the time and space to get to know each other better. I took Kirsty MacColl up on her invitation to lunch, bringing Kas with me. She realised she could almost claim credit for having brought us together, since it was her I'd been talking to at the very moment Kas and I had first noticed each other at Seb's memorial. Another moment of serendipity.

In May a street party was organised in Glengall Road to celebrate the fiftieth anniversary of VE Day. It was an extraordinary street on which to live owing to its eclectic mix of residents. There were artists, two doctors, a banker and a philosopher, all of whom had arrived with the gentrification of the area, not to isolate themselves in a middle-class ghetto but to integrate with the people who had lived there for years, like Marjorie, the redoubtable lady across the road from me who had spent the war there, dodging the bombs, even while pregnant. My lovely neighbours were surprised but enchanted by the new romance in their midst that had apparently come out of the blue. On that May afternoon we all dressed up in keeping with the occasion. I was Betty Grable and Kas, being an 'American', was a GI. Sara was there, too, with a couple of her friends, all looking gorgeous in forties-style frocks.

It was a blisteringly hot summer and we spent most of our free time having picnics in Holland Park and barbecues in the garden. On the Saturday morning of August Bank Holiday weekend, Sara and I were together in a hotel in West London. It seemed as though this was the day the weather might finally break. She zipped me into a pale lilac dress. Our hands were shaking slightly as we put on lipstick and primped our hair as we had done so many times before a party. But today the party was special. It was my wedding day.

A car arrived to take us to Glengall Road. There, over two hundred people were congregated in my garden – Mark's garden – extended for the day by my kindly next-door neighbours, who had temporarily taken down the fence between us. Among them were Kas's children Gabriel and Moon; Michelle and her husband, David; Jools and her partner, Richard, Debbie and Vicky, my assistant on *The Knowledge*; Adam and his family, all the way from France. The novelist Jon Fink, who had once written Michelle's name and number in my address book, was in attendance; Kirsty

MacColl arrived with a girlfriend. Aunt Bett, my cousin Danny and their family, Seb's mum and Mark's parents and friends were all there, too. The only person who couldn't make it was Tina, who was abroad with her husband. The ceremony was presided over by Father Tim, the same Irish priest who had conducted Seb's funeral. As I walked down an aisle created by long-stemmed flowers strewn on the lawn, Sara joined her two best friends, who waited for her in the front row of the 'congregation'. We exchanged a smile as I walked on to join my husband-to-be.

After the ceremony, looking beautiful in a white linen suit, holding down her hat in the summer breeze, Sara rose from her chair and came forward to read aloud a piece by Kahlil Gibran. She trembled a little as she held tightly to the piece of paper in her hand.

You were born together and together you shall be for evermore. You shall be together when the white wings of death scatter your days. Aye, you shall be together even in the silent memory of God. But let there be spaces in your togetherness, and let the winds of the heavens dance between you.

Music played – 'Will the Circle Be Unbroken' by the Staple Singers – and the sun shone on as we posed for the camera: a family photograph at long last.

Kas and I started our married life at Glengall Road, and I continued writing for television while he set up in London as a designer and builder, working on properties all over the city. Sara had started up her own actors' agency, with an office close to Oxford Street.

In April 1999, Kas and I bought a ramshackle little house in Whitstable on the east Kent coast. He did a lot of work on it, made it very comfortable and we began to base ourselves there, increasingly using the London flat as a *pied-à-terre* for visits and meetings. Sara would come down to see us in Whitstable, often bringing a friend along, but her work and relationships frequently kept her in London so sometimes it was easier for me to travel up and have lunch with her at a favourite small restaurant just around the corner from the BBC in Langham Street. By this time she was in her thirties and I, in my late forties, felt positively middle-aged.

The way in which my daughter and I had found each other seemed no less miraculous, but with the passage of time our relationship had found its own level.

I recognised now how all our lives are pierced with loss. In my case the greatest loss had been one of my own making. Yet in all the years since our meeting, Sara had never once reproached me for abandoning her as a baby. As I sat one day eating crêpes in that busy London restaurant, my daughter smiled at me across the table and I knew in that instant that, for all my youthful mistakes, I had been redeemed by love.

The years seemed to gallop by at a dizzying speed. On my fiftieth birthday Kas threw a party for me at Whitstable Castle. Sara wasn't able to come but I consoled myself for her absence with the words of the Gibran piece she had read at our wedding: 'Let there be spaces in your togetherness and let the winds of heaven dance between you'. Within a few years, she had given up her agency and changed direction, moving house to Middlesex. One evening she called to tell us that she had met someone, a man to whom she had become very close. I could tell from the sound of her voice that she was happy. That she was in love.

Life was busy for all of us. I was writing for two television drama series while Kas now had a workshop in Whitstable and never seemed to have a gap between jobs. But when we couldn't meet we kept in touch by phone and email. In no time at all, it seemed, it was 2007 and my daughter was calling with more dramatic news. 'Sit down,' she said, unable to keep the excitement from her voice. 'I've got something to tell you both.' She paused. 'I'm pregnant.'

I was over the moon for her. At thirty-seven, Sara was now the same age as I had been when she'd seen my name on a script at Hatton & Baker. My grown-up baby was going to have a baby herself. Could it possibly be true that, after spending such a large part of my life as a childless mother, I was now going to become a grandmother?

The pregnancy was problem-free – no morning sickness, no hypertension, no complications associated with Sara's age. She came to visit when she was six months' pregnant and didn't look very big at all. I remembered the kaftans I'd worn to hide my own small bump, transported back once more to the long months of denial, the mounting pressure of keeping my secret hidden. This pregnancy couldn't have been more different. Sara carried her unborn child with pride, and I gently laid my hands upon her belly, something my own mother had never had the chance to do with me. Although apprehensive about the labour itself, Sara was looking forward to the birth of her baby. She couldn't have been happier. For far too long she had mothered a brood of four cats – Charlie, Taz, Tommy Lee and Buster – just as I had done with Tiddles. Now it was time for her to make the shift from being an animal person to a children person.

On the morning of 28 February 2008, Sara went into labour. It was a leap year, and the next day would be a date that occurred only once every four years. Perhaps my daughter's baby would grow up disappointed not to have a proper birthday every year like everybody else, but I wasn't too bothered about that then. My mind was completely focused on Sara's welfare. It was a time to keep a respectful distance – her partner told us he would stay in touch throughout the labour and keep us fully informed – but I remained wide-eyed in bed that night, becoming a scared teenager again, alone in a hospital room, hearing the sounds of other women's screams around me. During my own labour, I had told myself that everything I felt was natural. I wasn't ill; I was going through a process. Everything would be all right and I would survive. Now I tried to send the same message to my daughter.

In the early hours of the morning, our telephone rang. Simultaneously a photograph suddenly sprang to life on Kas's mobile phone: a tiny, scrunched face stared back at us, tufty brown hair like a question-mark above his head. Caden Joseph had been born safe and well, and had escaped the leap year by just an hour.

The labour, however, had been difficult and Sara was kept in hospital, where she developed an infection. When Kas and I travelled up to London to see her, we found her looking jaundiced and weary. My heart went out to her, so much so that the baby to whom she had given birth remained secondary to my concerns for his mother. He lay quietly in her arms, sleeping, as though still exhausted from the sheer effort of being born. Sara moved slightly, opening her arms so that I could see his face.

Countless women had made this gesture to me over the years, proudly exhibiting a new member of their family. I knew only too well what usually came next: the invitation to hold another woman's baby. Many times I had managed to sidestep the offer. When obliged to comply, I had cradled the infant awkwardly, still wrenched by conflicted emotions. It was almost forty years since I had held my own baby daughter for the very last time before settling her into a nurse's arms. I had no idea how I would feel now having my daughter's child – my own grandson – placed into mine. Sara smiled tentatively.

'Would you like to hold him?'

I moved in closer. Caden, light as a feather, was suddenly in my embrace. He didn't cry; he didn't even wriggle. He lay quite still, as though trying to co-operate. Then his eyes suddenly opened, two bright blue buttons. Perhaps he was missing the smell of his mother because he blinked suspiciously before staring, unfocused, into the eyes of the stranger before him. I lowered my face towards him, breathing in the smell of my daughter's milk on his soft skin. All the years seemed suddenly to concertina into one moment. 'Welcome to the world,' I whispered to my grandson.

Since that day, I have thought many times of the crossroads that faced me as a young mother. Would it really have been impossible to have kept my baby and brought her up myself? Even with the wisdom of hindsight, I shall never know. The reality is, as little more than a child myself, I turned away from motherhood and chose instead another path. At times it was frightening and lonely, but I was blessed with friends, and I learned that, after a while, we grow tired of being scared. Yet I have also come to understand that we are all tied by blood and roots no matter how far we think we may have left them behind. Ultimately, we are the sum of all that came before us.

As a rebellious teenager I took a road less travelled but by some miracle, or some preordination, that road was to lead me to where I stand today, where I know I was always meant to be: with my daughter once again my life.

That has made all the difference.

Epilogue

In November 2010 it will be twenty years since my daughter handed me a cup of coffee without either of us knowing who the other was. Throughout that time I have written many dramatic plotlines, but none so extraordinary as the one that forever changed my own life that day.

I was often asked why I had never written my story. Until now, I never felt the time was right. I have always been careful not to infringe the 'copyright' of my daughter's life and feared that, if I were to choose the wrong moment or the wrong medium, I would be running the risk of exploiting what I have always considered to be a small miracle.

In January 2010 I was throwing out the Christmas newspapers when I came across an article entitled 'My Story'. It caught my attention, and I paused to read it. I learned that the BBC and the publishers HarperCollins were searching for special stories from ordinary people. I finally felt I had found the perfect way to tell this tale.

I discussed it with Sara, and she agreed that the time felt right. The only problem was that I now had only twenty-four hours to submit a proposal before the deadline for entries.

I sat down at my computer and words began to fill the screen. Given the severe weather and the backlog of Christmas mail, it was touch and go whether my submission would arrive in time. Somehow it did. Perhaps that, too, was a sign that it was meant to be.

Often in life we have to fight so hard against the flow to make things happen. We are told that nothing is won without effort, that we have to struggle for what we desire. But from my experience of finding Sara I have learned that, sometimes, things can work out by themselves. They just happen – and often for the best.

Over the years I have met other women who have been traumatised by the adoption process. I have been saddened, but not surprised, that many have been unable to share their experiences even with their own partners. Some have tried hard to be reconciled with their lost children and failed. A lot of them have gone on to have families at a later date, desperate to fill a vacuum too great to bear. I was never able to do that, but somehow I always knew that my daughter and I would meet again.

Now Sara is the mother of two children. Following an auspicious meeting in a not-so-far-flung pavilion, I feel blessed to have been granted a second chance: the opportunity to know and to love not only my lost daughter, but her own beautiful children, Caden and Tallulah.

May they all live happily ever after.

Acknowledgements

It would not have been possible for me to have written this book without the help, support and, indeed, the continuing presence in my life of some very special people. I would like to take this opportunity to thank them.

I am extremely grateful to Kate Mosse, Feargal Keane, Jenny Colgan and Kelly Webb-Lamb for choosing my story from among so many and for giving me the opportunity to tell it to a wider audience.

I am also indebted to Carole Tonkinson, Vicky McGeown and Helen Hawksfield at HarperCollins for their enthusiasm and their faultless judgement in putting me in contact with Caroline North, who employed buckets of talent, professionalism and sheer determination to ensure that this book was completed, miraculously, on time.

I will always be grateful to Adrian Hodges and Jon Fink for sending me on a path to Michelle Kass, who has not only supported me professionally for twenty years but was, indeed, the 'agent' in reuniting me with my long-lost daughter all those years ago. Michelle, you will always be our fairy godmother.

A big thank you to 'the girls': Julie Field, Tina Jamieson and Debbie Ellis, who were there at the crossroads, at just the right time, waiting to point me in a new direction.

Loving thanks go always to my 'pretend' family, Maureen and Sally Kjeldsen.

And to my husband, Kas, the love of my life, I give thanks for all your devotion to me, for your unfailing support – and for rushing off to the post box for me with more chapters.

Finally, I send love and gratitude to my absent friends, forever present in my heart: Maria Fernanda Celestina da Silva, Kay Peters, Mark Kjeldsen, 'Moes' Kjeldsen, Seb Harris, Kirsty MacColl, Theresa Wells, my 'Captain', Eric, and my dear old schoolfriend, June.